# Where the Water Hits the Wheel

# Where the Water Hits the Wheel

FIFTEEN SERMONS
ON THE GREAT BELIEFS OF THE CHRISTIAN FAITH

William G. Benton

Smyth & Helwys
Macon, Georgia
1993

# To my family,

## always there when I need them.

ISBN 1-880837-34-X

*Where the Water Hits the Wheel*
*Fifteen Sermons on the Great Beliefs of the Christian Faith*
Copyright © 1993
Smyth & Helwys Publishing, Inc.
1400 Coleman Avenue
Macon, Georgia 31207

Scripture quotations, unless otherwise noted, are from the New International Version Copyright © 1978 by New York International Bible Society and are used by permission.

The paper used in this publication exceeds the minimum requirements of American National Standard for Information requirements of American National Standard for Information Sciences—Permanence of Paper for Printed Library Materials, ANSI Z39.48–1984.

*Library of Congress Cataloging-in-Publication Data*

Benton, William G.
    Where the water hits the wheel : fifteen sermons on the great beliefs of the Christian faith / William G. Benton.
        viii + 127 pages     15 x 23 cm.     6 x 9"
    ISBN 1-880837-34-X (alk. paper)
    1. Theology, Doctrinal—Sermons. 2. Sermons, American.
I. Title
BT80.B44 1993
252—dc20                                                     93-3849
                                                                  CIP

# Contents

# Preface

When I was a first year seminary student, life was filled with Greek, Church History, Old Testament and New Testament classes—and fore–boding. The word was out that the required second year's Systematic Theology was a real bear. We were told to get prepared for a rough year.

My fear began to subside, however, after a conversation with the Systematic Theology professor, Dr. John Eddins. Excited about his subject, he said, "This is where the water hits the wheel." I took his class the next year and came to share his love for theology. After all, Systematic Theology was basically a course about how we think about God and what we believe as Christians.

Since my first pastorate I have wanted to preach a sermon series that would bring the great truths of our faith home to the people in the pew. I wanted Christians to be able to grasp the basics of our beliefs, to know what we stand for, even to share in the joy of Systematic Theology.

I kept putting off the idea, however, wanting always to read the latest work on the subject. Finally, the water hit the wheel in another sense. I developed kidney cancer and began what has become a seven-year struggle for life itself. Several months ago it became clear that if I were ever going to preach on the great beliefs, I'd better get started. I sat down with David Helms, a colleague with a good mind and a shared love for these things, and came up with a list of sermons that would be appropriate for the series. We began with thirteen titles and ended up with fifteen sermons, each of them produced in the face of the spreading and sometimes debilitating cancer. It has often seemed that I was in a race with time, though the drive to finish the project supplied me with much of the fortitude needed to see it through. At the completion of the last sermon I turned to one of our members, Mrs. Kathy Whiteside, to help me get all the material in a form the publisher could use. I would never have gotten it done without her diligence.

As you read these sermons bear in mind the audience for which they are intended—lay people who want to know more about the nuts and bolts of our faith, believers who want to know what it is we really believe.

Because the battle to finish the job and the battle to continue life have been interwoven from the beginning, I asked the publisher if we could include as a closing the sermon "A Good Theology for Bad Times." It seems to have meant something to folks dealing with pain or death. Maybe it tells better than any of the others where the water hits the wheel.

William G. Benton
February 22, 1993
York, South Carolina

# 1
# Great Beliefs of the Christian Faith:
## GOD THE FATHER

*Psalm 95:1-7*

[1]Come, let us sing for joy to the Lord; let us shout aloud to the Rock of our salvation.
[2]Let us come before him with thanksgiving and extol him with music and song.
[3]For the Lord is the great God, the great king above all gods.
[4]In his hand are the depths of the earth, and the mountain peaks belong to him.
[5]The sea is his, for he made it, and his hands formed the dry land.
[6]Come, let us bow down in worship, let us kneel before the Lord our Maker;
[7]for he is our God and we are the people of his pasture, the flock under his care.

*1 Peter 1:3-5*

[3]Praise be to the God and Father of our Lord Jesus Christ! In his great mercy he has given us new birth into a living hope through the resurrection of Jesus Christ from the dead, [4]and into an inheritance that can never perish, spoil or fade—kept in heaven for you, [5]who through faith are shielded by God's power until the coming of the salvation that is ready to be revealed in the last time.

*Hosea 11*

"When Israel was a child, I loved him, and out of Egypt I called my son. [2]But the more I called Israel, the further they went from me. They sacrificed to the Baals and they burned incense to images. [3]It was I who taught Ephraim to walk, taking them by the arms; but they did not realize it was I who healed them. [4]I led them with cords of human kindness, with ties of love; I lifted the yoke from their neck and bent down to feed them. [5]"Will they not return to Egypt and will not Assyria rule over them because they refuse to repent? [6]Swords will flash in their cities, will destroy the bars of their gates and put an end to their plans. [7]My people are determined to turn from me. Even if they call to the Most High, he will by no means exalt them. [8]"How can I give you up, Ephraim? How can I hand you over, Israel? How can I treat you like Admah? How can I make you like Zeboiim? My heart is changed within me; all my compassion is aroused. [9]I will not carry out my fierce anger, nor will I turn and devastate Ephraim. For I am God, and not man—the Holy One among you. I will not come in wrath. [10]They will follow the Lord; he will roar like a lion. When he roars, his children will come trembling from the west. [11]They will come trembling like birds from Egypt, like doves from Assyria. I will settle them in their homes," declares the Lord.

An English preacher began his sermon to a congregation in India with the sentence, "Now faith is both abstract and concrete." His interpreter translated: "So far the minister hasn't said anything, but when he does I'll let you know."

I hope these sermons on the Great Beliefs of the Christian Faith won't leave you feeling that the minister hasn't said anything or perhaps worse has said what nobody understands. My goal throughout is to talk about what we believe as Christians, and to do so in a way that will help us to understand, in a way that will clarify, and perhaps even answer some questions we've had in mind.

One of the first things you have to decide when you study the Christian faith is where to begin. Some people begin with the Bible. In fact, the *Baptist Faith and Message* begins with the Bible. But that is not the best place to start for several reasons. For one thing the Bible did not come first. Not only did God come before the Bible, but so did the Christian faith. The only scriptures the church had in the beginning were the Jewish scriptures, the Old Testament. By the time the Bible came to include the New Testament as we know it, the church had spread out of the Middle East and across the Mediterranean.

For another thing, to begin with the Bible is to assign first place and, therefore, first importance to something other than God. And anytime anybody or anything comes before God we are likely to be guilty of idolatry.

Then some people begin their study of theology with the doctrine of humanity. In other words they begin with the indisputable fact that human beings exist, and move out from there to draw further conclusions about reality. The English essayist Alexander Pope was of this persuasion. He wrote, "Know then thyself, presume not God to scan, for the proper study of mankind is man."

While it may seem perfectly logical to some people to begin with ourselves, it seems to me again to put the emphasis in the wrong place.

So we begin with God. The Bible begins with God ("In the beginning God . . ."). We believe that all of life and all that is came from God. We believe that before everything else and after everything else God is. Perhaps the Swiss theologian Emil Brunner put it best in one of my favorite quotations: "God is not in the world, the world is in God."

So we begin with God, and specifically with God the Father. And what can we say we believe about God the Father? Let me suggest that we use as an outline a portion of one of the simple little blessings that most of us learned as children, and that many of us hear around the dinner table everyday. It goes like this: "God is great, God is good. Let us thank him for our food." Here you see affirmed three very important facts about God the Father. God is great. God is good. And God is personal—that is to say, we can relate to Him and He to us.

I.

When we say "God is great" we are thinking of great in its older sense of big or grand. God is big. He is bigger than we can imagine. He is so grand as to be without comparison, and so powerful as to be unintimidated and unthreatened by anything at all.

The biblical writers are forever pointing us to the bigness, the grandeurs of God, in both the Old and New Testaments. The Psalmist writes, "I will exalt you, my God the King . . . Great is the Lord and most worthy of praise; his greatness no one can fathom." (Psalm 145).

And Paul writes in Romans, ". . . I am convinced that neither height nor depth, nor anything else in all creation, will be able to separate us from the love of God . . ." (Rom 8:38-39).

Do you see what a big God we serve? He is big enough to have created all that is, and big enough to have become involved in that creation.

Several years ago I heard a story that illustrates the greatness of God. A law firm in New York had been engaged to get a clear title on some property in New Orleans. They asked a New Orleans law firm to take care of the matter, and they did, tracing the title back to 1803. The New York firm responded that this was not going far enough back. This is the response they received:

"Gentlemen: Please be advised that in the year 1803 the United States of America acquired the territory of Louisiana from the Republic of France by purchase. The Republic of France had acquired title from the Spanish crown by conquest, the Spanish crown having obtained it by virtue of the discoveries of one Christopher Columbus, a Genoese sailor, who had been authorized to embark by Isabella, Queen of Spain, who obtained sanction from the Pope, the Vicar of Christ, who is the Son and heir of Almighty God, who made Louisiana!"

## II.

The second truth about God the Father is as important as the first—God is great, but He is also good. The first tells us something about the power of God, the second something about the nature of God.

It is important to have the right picture of the nature of God. Some people have a wrong picture of God and, therefore, a mistaken theology. Some, for example, see only the power of God and emphasize his omnipotence. But a God who is all–powerful could just as well be a celestial tyrant, playing with our lives and our fates for his own amusement.

Some people picture God in just the opposite sort of way, as an old and disabled creator who has done what he's going to do and is now watching things run their course.

And some see God as a kind of diffuse force that is to be identified with nature.

Against these distorted views we accept the biblical ideas of God as great, and good, and personal.

The biblical writers present the goodness of God in many ways. The Psalmist wrote of God as a shepherd who cares for his sheep. Jesus told a parable that pictured God as the loving, patient father who waited to receive the prodigal son when he finally returned home. The prophet Hosea pictured God as a mother caring for an infant:

> When Israel was a child I loved him, and out of Egypt I called my son. But the more I called Israel the further they went from me. It was I who taught Ephraim to walk. I lifted the yoke from their neck and bent down to feed them. (Then, after disappointment that so many parents feel.) How can I give you up, Ephraim? How can I hand you over Israel? I will not carry out my fierce anger, for I am God, and not man.

Perhaps a reasonable picture of the goodness of God is to reflect on the warm love of parents or even grandparents. I came across an essay written by a third-grader, entitled, "What's a Grandmother?"

"A grandmother is a lady who has no children of her own. She likes other people's little girls and boys. A grandfather is a man grandmother. He goes for walks with the boys and they talk about fishing and stuff like that.

Grandmothers don't have to do anything except to be there. They're old so they shouldn't play hard or run. It is enough if they drive us to the market where the pretend horse is and have a lot of dimes ready. Or if they take us for walks, they should slow down past things like pretty leaves and caterpillars. They should never say, 'Hurry up.'

Usually grandmothers are fat, but not too fat to tie your shoes. They wear glasses and funny underwear. They can take their teeth and gums off.

Grandmothers don't have to be smart, only answer questions like, 'Why isn't God married?' and 'How come dogs chase cats?'

Grandmothers don't talk baby talk like visitors do, because it is hard to understand. When they read to us they don't skip or mind if it is the same story over again.

Everybody should try to have a grandmother, especially if you don't have television, because they are the only grown-ups who have time."

That may be a cute picture of a grandmother, but through the innocent eyes of a child we catch without mistake the presence of a love and of a goodness that reflects in some ways how the biblical writers felt about God. God is great, but he is also good.

## III.

The third thing to note about God the Father is that God is personal. He wants not only to be praised and obeyed. He also wants a relationship with us. When the late Bob Benson was on a local television talk show, he was rather taken aback when the host opened by asking, "If there were one thing you could tell the audience today, what would it be?" Benson thought just a moment and then gave a seven-word answer: "God has something to say to you." And he added that if he could say one more thing it would be, "You will hear Him if you listen."

That kind of affirmation goes to the heart of the biblical faith. God is not just "out there"; He is here with us. Harry Emerson Fosdick said that a God who doesn't care doesn't count, but this God goes to great lengths to let us know that He does care for us, He does know us. If the hairs on our head are numbered, if He stands at the door and knocks, surely our pain, frustrations, and hopes are known to Him. That's because God is that kind of God.

One of the great thinkers in Christian history was the Frenchman Blaise Pascal. When he died in 1662 it was found that he had stitched into his coat, between the cloth and lining so that it would be next to his heart, a piece of paper and on this piece of paper he had written about his conversion experience. Among the words were these: "God of Abraham, God of Isaac, God of Jacob, not of the philosophers and scholars. I know. I know. I feel joy and peace."

Pascal has given us a worthy testimony about the God we worship. He is not found at the end of an equation or as the result of a philosophical argument. He is alive. He relates to people. He is waiting this morning for us too to say, "Yes, Father, you are my God." And where could you find a better one?

# 2
# Great Beliefs of the Christian Faith:
## THE INCARNATION

*John 1:1-5, 14*

¹In the beginning was the Word, and the Word was with God, and the Word was God. ²He was with God in the beginning. ³Through him all things were made; without him nothing was made that has been made. ⁴In him was life, and that life was the light of men. ⁵The light shines in the darkness, but the darkness has not understood it.

¹⁴The Word became flesh and made his dwelling among us. We have seen his glory, the glory of the One and Only, who came from the Father, full of grace and truth.

When we talk about God the Son we are dealing with the Incarnation, which means that God has come in the flesh in Jesus Christ. The word "incarnation" means in the flesh. You have heard someone remark, "That boy is the incarnation of his father," meaning it's like seeing his father all over again. Some people believe in re-incarnation, which is the idea that after you die you will return to live again in another body, or in the flesh.

Now there are two questions we need to deal with this morning. First, we need to ask who Jesus was; and second, we need to ask what Jesus did.

## I.

It seems a simple question at first, "Who was Jesus of Nazareth?" But that question has troubled people through all the centuries since Jesus lived. The early church had trouble with it, even the disciples. It is only after we are half-way through the Gospel of Mark that Peter confesses, "You are the Christ." It was several hundred years later that the church realized that Jesus was fully human and fully divine.

If you read the Gospels, you have no trouble seeing that Jesus was human. The writers are careful to show that he got hungry and thirsty, just as you and I do; that he was impatient with some people; and that he was tempted in the same ways we are. It is a very human Jesus who leaps off the pages of scripture. Perhaps one of the most significant remarks about the human Jesus comes from Luke, who wrote that Jesus grew in wisdom. Like us, he learned as he grew older and he benefitted from experience.

Now what does it mean that Jesus was human? It means that God has put on flesh and faced life as we face it. It is really difficult to enter into another person's experience. Last week I read a book entitled *I Know Why the Caged Bird Sings*, by the black woman writer Maya Angelou. It tells of her growing up as a black person in the South back in the 30s and 40s. Although we may know some of the facts of life as black people lived it, it is only through the eyes of someone like Angelou that we can really begin to appreciate what it was like to be black. She tells of an occasion when she was 8 or 10 years old and had a terrible toothache. Her grandmother generally took care of these matters with some string and some strength, but this was a particularly bad case. So the grandmother got herself and her granddaughter bathed and dressed in their best and walked into the white section of town and up the back stairway of the dentist's office.

As it turned out, the dentist had borrowed some money from her in the past, so he knew who she was. When the nurse said, "Annie wants to see you," he stepped to the back door. The grandmother explained the situation and how she would not have come except for the extreme agony of her grandchild. Unmoved by the woman's pleas, the dentist asserted, "Annie, do you know what a policy is? Well, I have a policy; I don't work on black people's teeth." The grandmother moved the situation a notch higher, reminding the dentist that it wasn't for herself that she was asking, but for her grandchild, and that she had been accommodating when he had needed help. He finally shut the case and the door, saying,

"Annie, I won't do it and that's final. I'd rather stick my hand in a dog's mouth."

Now can anybody here know what that kind of rejection must have felt like? We can't unless we could somehow enter the world of the black community. Well, God has entered the world of the human community by becoming human like we are, facing what we face, even to the point of dying a horrible death. Because Jesus was fully human, we know that God knows our feelings and frustrations, that he understands what we face.

II.

The second thing we need to say about who Jesus was is that he was divine. He was God-in-the-flesh. When Philip asked Jesus to show them the Father, Jesus replied, "Anyone who has seen me has seen the Father."

While some people have trouble believing that Jesus was really human, there are others who have trouble believing that he was really God-in-the-flesh. I've had numerous conversations across the years with people who would say something to the effect that Jesus was a great moral teacher, a wonderful example, a special kind of person, or the last of the great prophets—the likes of another Isaiah, Jeremiah, or Ezekiel.

But to make that claim is to make nonsense of virtually all that the New Testament tells us. First, if the Son of Man was not also the Son of God, then he was a first-rate fraud because he certainly claimed that status. None of the prophets ever claimed to be such. They may have felt that they could point the way, speak the truth, and encourage life, but none of them dared say, as Jesus did, "I am the way, the truth, and the life."

If the Son of Man was not also the Son of God, then the apostles surely died for a poor cause. Do you think for a moment that they would have sacrificed all they had, spread out to distant lands, and faced hardships and finally death—would they have done that for an Isaiah, great as he was?

Of course not. The simple truth is that Jesus was who he said he was, or else our whole faith is founded on a sham, and we of all people are most to be pitied.

Do you recall the story I told a couple of weeks ago on Wednesday night? During the French Revolution, M. Lepeau invented a completely new religion—a rational, sensible religion that he felt the people could accept. When his new religion found no great audience, he complained to Talleyrand, who suggested, "If you want your religion to catch on, why don't you try getting yourself crucified and then rise from the dead three days later!"

Of all the religious leaders who have ever lived and taught, all the prophets, the shamans, the great moral teachers—of only one can it be said that he arose from the dead. And that one is Jesus, both the Son of Man and the Son of God.

### III.

The first question concerning the Incarnation is who Jesus was. The second involves what Jesus did. Here is God–who–has–come–in–the–flesh. What does that do for us? It does two things.

First, it gives us an example to follow. It gives us the standard of life as God intended it to be lived. Jesus showed us by his life what it means to love God with all our heart, strength, and mind; and what it means to love our neighbor as ourselves. He showed us what it means to go the second mile, and to turn the other cheek. He showed us what it means to forgive when he faced his own tormentors and said, "Father, forgive them."

Some might say at this point that the standard is impossibly high. Of course no one could live as Jesus lived. But the truth is that most of us could come closer to it if we tried.

A committee once asked the great tenor Enrico Caruso to sing at a concert that would benefit a charity. The chairman said, "Of course, Mr. Caruso, as this is a charity event we would not expect much from you. Your name alone will draw a crowd and you can merely sing some song requiring little effort or skill." Caruso replied firmly: "Gentlemen, Caruso never does less than his best."

When we carry the name of Christ, which is what we do when

we call ourselves Christians, then we, too, should settle for nothing less than our best, and even then we should continue to grow into the fullness of the measure of our Lord.

IV.

What did Jesus do? First, he set an example by his life. Then he purchased our redemption by his death. In other words, Jesus did something for us by dying on the cross. Both the Scriptures and the church through the ages have expressed this truth in a number of ways. Paul explained it this way: God made him who had no sin (Jesus) to become sin for us so that we might receive the righteousness of God. By accepting Jesus's death on our behalf, our sins are forgiven, and we truly become children of God.

There are many ways to illustrate this truth, none of them quite covering all that Jesus's death on the cross encompasses. This week I came across an account of a father and son riding down the road together when a bee flew into the car. The boy was extremely allergic to bee stings and became quite agitated. His father, realizing the seriousness of the situation, reached out and grabbed the bee. He held it for a few seconds in his hand, then let it go. The boy was still afraid, until the father showed him his hand with the stinger in it and explained that the bee could now do him no harm.

Think, if you will, of Jesus on the cross with his outstretched hands and the nails in them. Those nails signify that death and sin can no longer bring us harm. The sting has been taken out of them on the cross. That's why we sing,

> When I survey the wondrous cross,
> On which the Prince of glory died,
> My richest gain I count but loss,
> And pour contempt on all my pride.
>
> Forbid it, Lord, that I should boast,
> Save in the death of Christ my God;

All the vain things that charm me most,
I sacrifice them to his blood.

See, from his head, his hands, his feet,
Sorrow and love flow mingled down;
Did e'er such love and sorrow meet,
Or thorns compose so rich a crown.

Were the whole realm of nature mine,
That were a present far too small;
Love so amazing, so divine,
Demands my soul, my life, my all.

# 3
# Great Beliefs of the Christian Faith:
# GOD THE HOLY SPIRIT

*Ezekiel 37:1-10*

[1]The hand of the Lord was upon me, and he brought me out by the Spirit of the Lord and set me in the middle of a valley; it was full of bones. [2]He led me back and forth among them, and I saw a great many bones on the floor of the valley, bones that were very dry. [3]He asked me, "Son of man, can these bones live?" I said, "O Sovereign Lord, you alone know." [4]Then he said to me, "Prophesy to these bones and say to them, 'Dry bones, hear the word of the Lord! [5]This is what the Sovereign Lord says to these bones: I will make breath enter you, and you will come to life. [6]I will attach tendons to you and make flesh come upon you and cover you with skin; I will put breath in you, and you will come to life. Then you will know that I am the Lord.'" [7]So I prophesied as I was commanded. And as I was prophesying, there was a noise, a rattling sound, and the bones came together, bone to bone. [8]I looked, and tendons and flesh appeared on them and skin covered them, but there was no breath in them. [9]Then he said to me, "Prophesy to the breath; prophesy, son of man, and say to it, 'This is what the Sovereign Lord says: Come from the four winds, O breath, and breathe into these slain, that they may live.'" [10]So I prophesied as he commanded me, and breath entered them; they came to life and stood up on their feet—a vast army.

*Acts 2:42-47*

[42]They devoted themselves to the apostles' teaching and to the fellowship, to the breaking of bread and to prayer. [43]Everyone was filled with awe, and many wonders and miraculous signs were done by the apostles. [44]All the believers were together and had everything in common. [45]Selling their possessions and goods, they gave to anyone as he had need. [46]Every day they continued to meet together in the temple courts. They broke bread in their homes and ate together with glad and sincere hearts, [47]praising God and enjoying the favor of all the people. And the Lord added to their number daily those who were being saved.

*Galatians 5:22-23*

[22]But the fruit of the Spirit is love, joy, peace, patience, kindness, goodness, faithfulness, [23]gentleness and self-control. Against such things there is no law.

Our examination of the Great Beliefs of the Christian Faith has already led us to consider God the Father and God the Son—the Incarnation. Our focus now turns to God the Holy Spirit. The subject is much bigger than a single sermon can do justice to. In fact, if you go to seminary, you can take an entire course on the Holy Spirit. And if you go to a theological book store, you will find many books on the subject of the Holy Spirit.

What I hope to do today is to provide an introduction to the subject that deals with two questions: briefly with the question, Who is the Holy Spirit?, and more fully with the question, What does the Holy Spirit do?

I.

First, Who is the Holy Spirit? Simply put, the Holy Spirit is another way of saying God. It is important to remember as Christians that we do *not* believe in three Gods, but rather in one God who expresses or manifests Himself in three ways: as God the Father, God the Son (Jesus Christ), and God the Holy Spirit.

There is no perfect analogy to explain how this can be so, but two examples may help us to grasp the truth of the Trinity. One theologian put it this way: I am to my parents a son, to my wife a husband, to my children a father—but I am still only one person! Similarly, the Bible refers to God and to God's activity in various ways, but it is still one God to whom we refer. Whether He is called Creator, Holy Spirit, the Christ, the Spirit of Jesus (a phrase Paul used on one occasion), or the Good Shepherd, it is still one God who has expressed himself through the ages in various ways.

Someone suggested comparing the Trinity to a natural

phenomenon with which all of us are familiar—water. Water, or $H_2O$, comes in three forms. As a liquid it is water, as a solid it is ice, and as a gas it is steam. But water, ice, and steam are all $H_2O$.

So bear in mind as we study the Holy Spirit we are focusing *not* on a different God, but on a different form or expression of the one God.

## II.

Now, what does the Holy Spirit do? I have chosen three texts to illustrate the work of the Holy Spirit, and the first one is Ezekiel 37 in the Old Testament. The reason I begin there is to be certain you understand that the Holy Spirit is not just a New Testament experience, but a reality that goes back to the beginning. In fact, if you start reading in Genesis, you only get to the second verse before you meet the Spirit of God hovering over the waters.

The Ezekiel passage teaches us the first important fact about the Holy Spirit: *He gives life.* Just as the Spirit breathed life into the dry bones in Ezekiel's vision, so today the indwelling of the Holy Spirit is what gives us life.

In England there is a paper factory that makes the finest stationery you can buy anywhere in the world. A tourist who was being shown through the plant by a guide wondered at a large pile of rags that he saw—dirty, worn, discarded rags. The guide explained that these rags went into the paper so that the higher the rag content the finer the paper. The tourist ordered some stationery for himself; and when he received it several weeks later the company's slogan was stamped on the box: "Dirty rags transformed."

That is what the work of the Holy Spirit does in our lives. Isaiah spoke of our righteousness as filthy rags. Well, God's Spirit fills us and transforms us so that our rags become the stationery on which he can write his word and his will. Paul said, "It is God who works in you to will and to do." This is what he was talking about.

A. J. Gordon was out in the country one day when he saw across a field an old hand-operated water pump and a farmer who was pumping for all he was worth. What amazed Gordon was the vitality and strength of this farmer. He watched him pump the water, never seeming to tire or to get off routine. He decided to go speak to the farmer. So he headed out across the field with the farmer furiously pumping, never missing a beat. When he got to the pump, however, the mystery was solved. The "farmer" was a plywood figure that someone had cut out and placed at the pump, and the pump itself was an artesian well that ran constantly.

So what was actually happening was the opposite of what appeared to be happening. The farmer wasn't pumping the water; the water was pumping the farmer.

When Jesus tells the woman at the well about living water that wells up in you to eternal life, he was talking about this wonderful reality of the Holy Spirit: He gives life. He dwells within and drives the pump. He even breathes into our weary failed bones, into our cemeteries of dreams and hopes—and gives life. That is the first work of the Holy Spirit.

III.

What does the Holy Spirit do? First, He gives life. Second, the Holy Spirit creates community. Listen to the account in the Book of Acts of what happens to the Christian Community after Pentecost (Acts 2:42-47). Obviously these people have experienced something in their lives that has given them a new set of priorities and a new sense of community.

Just throwing people together doesn't make community. Years ago when rural families lived miles apart they invariably knew who their neighbors were. Today people who live in high–rise apartments often know nothing of those who spend their lives only a few feet away or just down the hall. It takes more than close proximity to create community. Think of the last time you were in a crowded elevator. Do you remember how awkward it felt. Here we are pushing up against people—but still no sense of community.

The Holy Spirit creates community. He brings people together; He tears down walls that separate; He makes something like a family out of people who may not have anything much in common except their Christian faith.

When we were in North Carolina, we had a family come into our church who had previously been uninvolved in any church. In fact, I baptized both the husband and the wife. Later, after we'd moved away, we received word that the lady's father had died suddenly and unexpectedly. I called her to express sympathy and was a bit startled when she said she had a question she wanted to ask. I began to imagine that she would ask about why these things happen, or why God didn't prevent untimely death. I was prepared for something difficult. This is what she asked: "How in the world do people make it through times like these without a church? Thank God," she said, "for our church."

How many of us today could testify in the same way to what the church has meant to us in times of birth or death or illness. And what is the church but the community of believers brought together by the Holy Spirit. Think about it: First Baptist Church is not a church because we're all going to vote the same way in the presidential election, or because we all agree on issues such as abortion or capital punishment. We are not a political community. We are a spiritual community created by the Holy Spirit.

A group of Boy Scouts were out in the woods exploring one day. They came across a set of railroad tracks and began to try to walk them. If you've ever tried to maintain your balance on a slippery rail, you know how they felt and how far they got. But two smart guys assured the rest that they could walk the rails at least 100 feet without falling. Nobody believed them, so they had to prove it. And of course they did it by helping each other. Each stood on a rail and then they reached out their arms and locked them together. The two walked down the tracks without falling off.

The community created by the Holy Spirit is one that can walk the rails, too. We hold on to and depend upon each other.

IV.

The third thing the Holy Spirit does is to produce fruit in the believer's life. Paul says in Galatians 5:22-23 that "the fruit of the

Spirit is love, joy, peace, patience, kindness, goodness, faithfulness, gentleness and self–control." Jesus had said that you can tell a tree by the fruit it bears. And Paul says, in effect, well, here is the fruit you bear if the Holy Spirit lives in you. That's a pretty inclusive list. In fact, if we look at ourselves in light of it, we'll probably conclude that we're not bearing all the fruit that God intended.

The point is, though, that a Christian ought to be different. If the Holy Spirit lives in you, it ought to show.

Luis Palau, a South American evangelist, tells of a woman in Peru whose life was radically transformed when she became a Christian. Rosario, a terrorist and an expert in martial arts, had killed twelve policemen. When she heard that Luis Palau was conducting a crusade in Lima, Peru, she determined to make her way to the stadium to kill him. When she got to the stadium, she had to listen to the message because it took some time to work her way to the speaker. By the time she did so, the message had worked its way into her heart, and she became a Christian.

When Luis Palau saw her ten years later, listen to what she had done. She had assisted in the planting of five churches, had founded an orphanage to house over one thousand children, and was still working hard as a witness and a worker in the church.

You see, before she became a Christian and the Holy Spirit came into her life, she had born fruit—hatred, violence, murder. And after the Holy Spirit came in, she still bore fruit, but of a completely different kind: love, joy, peace, patience, kindness, goodness, faithfulness, gentleness and self-control.

So the Holy Spirit does three things. First, He gives life. And who could ever forget that powerful picture Ezekiel paints of dried bones that come to life because the Spirit breathes on them. Second, He creates community. And who can forget that picture in Acts of such selfless living and giving in the early church. And third, He bears fruit in the believer. Who cannot marvel at the difference between before and after.

How is it with you? Have you ever invited the Spirit into your life? If not, what are you waiting for?

# 4
# Great Beliefs of the Christian Faith:
# REVELATION—
# HOW DO WE KNOW ABOUT GOD?

*Acts 14:15-17*

[15]"Men, why are you doing this? We too are only men, human like you. We are bringing you good news, telling you to turn from these worthless things to the living God, who made heaven and earth and sea and everything in them. [16]In the past, he let all nations go their own way. [17]Yet he has not left himself without testimony: He has shown kindness by giving you rain from heaven and crops in their seasons; he provides you with plenty of food and fills your hearts with joy."

*2 Timothy 3:16-17*

[16]All Scripture is God-breathed and is useful for teaching, rebuking, correcting and training in righteousness, [17]so that the man of God may be thoroughly equipped for every good work.

*2 Kings 2:23-25*

[23]From there Elisha went up to Bethel. As he was walking along the road, some youths came out of the town and jeered at him. "Go on up, you baldhead!" they said. "Go on up, you baldhead!." [24]He turned around, looked at them and called down a curse on them in the name of the Lord. Then two bears came out of the woods and mauled forty-two of the youth. [25]And he went on to Mount Carmel and from there returned to Samaria.

*Colossians 1:19*

[19]For God was pleased to have all his fullness dwell in him.

This sermon is about the doctrine of revelation, not the Book of Revelation. The question is, How do we know about God? Most of us don't give much thought to that question. For us, knowing about God and believing in God are about as natural as breathing.

But suppose you're talking with someone at work and she wants to know why you believe the way you do. Or suppose a neighbor is visiting and he says, "I know there's got to be something more to life than I'm seeing, someone bigger than I am—but who is it, what is it, and how do I know for sure?" Could you explain to that person how we know about God? Or maybe in some hour of personal crisis or trial, or a time of doubt, or spiritual drought, you even wonder yourself: How do we know about God, what God is like, and that he cares for us?

That is what we want to consider this morning. The first thing we need to understand is that we know about God *not* because we have discovered Him, but because He has revealed Himself to us. God was not found at the end of a chemistry equation, nor at the edge of the universe, nor through the mind of a philosopher or mystic. God was not found; He showed himself. He *revealed* Himself to us (hence the word revelation). Jesus said, "You did not choose me; I chose you." To paraphrase that, we did not discover God, or think up God, or invent God. God came to us. He showed himself to us, and he has done this primarily in four ways.

I.

First, God reveals Himself in nature. There's an interesting story from Paul's first missionary journey reported in Acts 14. It occurs in a place called Lystra. Following a healing the people rush to worship Paul and Barnabas as gods. Paul, of course, used the occasion to preach a sermon. Listen to what he says:

We are bringing you good news . . . from the living God who made heaven and earth and sea and everything in them. He has not left himself without testimony: He has shown kindness by giving you rain from heaven and crops in their seasons; He provides you with plenty of food and fills your heart with joy.

The essence of Paul's sermon is to show from our experiences of nature that there must be a God. We can plant the crop, but we can't make it grow; we can put the seed in the ground, but we can't make it rain. We can't even make the sunshine come up tomorrow though we are fairly certain that it will.

Now we could spend the rest of the day talking about the complexities of nature. We can make a hearing aid, but we can't make an ear. We can make contact lens, but we can't make an eye. The world we live in is so complex and so full of testimonies that something or someone far beyond us, far above us, has put his mark on it.

I can give you a personal illustration from recent surgery. The surgeon put in a gastric tube—a plastic tube about as round as your smallest finger, running from inside the stomach, all the way through the body, to the outside, where it was stitched in place so it would stay put. The tube could be used for either of two purposes: for draining the stomach or for feeding. The thing that concerned me, however, was what would happen when they took the tube out. How were they going to plug the hole in the stomach and on the outside of the body? In fact I asked the surgeon when he went to remove it: "Can you guarantee me that I won't just deflate or have a blow–out like a tire when you take this out?" He smiled and said, "Don't worry. Your body knows just what to do. Within two hours it will begin sealing itself off and within a few days you won't even have any drainage."

Once again we encounter in nature the proof that there is something or someone out there, or in here, far bigger than we are. The surgeon can make the cut, but he can't make it heal.

But there is another side to nature. We need to be honest with the facts. The same nature that gives our bodies remarkable healing powers, and that gives us beautiful mountainsides in the fall—that same nature also gives us Hurricane Andrew and tornadoes that seem to strike out of nowhere. How do we square that with the idea that nature is evidence that God is at work? Well, we see that nature doesn't give us a perfect picture of God—so we move on.

## II.

God reveals himself through nature. He also reveals himself through the Bible. 2 Timothy 3:16-17 says, "All scripture is God-breathed (inspired) and is useful for teaching, rebuking, correcting, and training in righteousness." That means that God speaks to us through the Scriptures. He speaks to our happy times and to our sad times. We read the beautiful love chapter from I Corinthians when we join two people in marriage. We read the shepherd's psalm when we comfort a family in grief. And when we read the Scriptures, we hear God speaking through them if we listen.

The story has often been repeated about the German theologian Karl Barth coming to visit America. Barth had written an incredible systematic theology—thick volumes of small print dealing with God. One of the press asked Barth if he could state his basic theology in a sentence! Think of that: years of research, writing, thinking—volumes of work—in a sentence. The crusty old theologian paused for a moment and then replied, "Jesus loves me, this I know, for the Bible tells me so." In a way, Barth was playing games with them. But in another way he was giving the testimony of a lifetime of work, saying in effect, what I know, I know because the Bible has told me so.

L. D. Johnson was one of the heroes of my college years. He was chaplain at Furman University. Dr. Johnson developed cancer at about the time he retired and fought a valiant struggle for several years. After he died, the assistant chaplain told me that near the end, Johnson had asked for a book. "Which book?" his friend inquired. Johnson replied, "At this point in a man's life there is only one book."

Through the Scriptures God reveals himself, but we must again be honest about the facts. Just as nature is not a perfect picture of God, neither are the Scriptures. There is much in them that does not bring us comfort or understanding, but just makes us wonder, What in the world is going on here?

I was teaching a Bible Study in a church several years ago when somebody asked me, "Preacher, what do you do with a passage like 2 Kings 2:23-25?" Off the top of my head I didn't know what the passage referred to, so we turned to it and I read it. Some youths had called Elisha a baldhead and he "called down a curse on them in the name of the Lord." Then two bears came out of the woods and mauled forty–two of the youths.

I told the fellow that there were many things I did not understand and I filed them away in a part of my mind called "awaiting further light." At the same time, I explained, we don't worship the kind of God who would send bears to maul children because they called somebody a name. How do I know that?

### III.

Because God has revealed Himself in a third way: He has come in the flesh and his name is Jesus. The best answer *always* to what God is like is to point to Jesus Christ. There we see the perfect expression of God's will and God's way. Much of the theology that is practiced today in the pews and in the parlor misses the mark because it stops with nature or with the Bible and doesn't go on to the fullest revelation we have of God, which is in Jesus Christ our Lord. Paul puts it this way in Colossians 1:19, "God was pleased to have all his fullness dwell in him"—and listen to the effect of that—"and through him to reconcile all things to himself . . . by making peace through his blood, shed on the cross."

We need to measure our theology by Jesus before we pronounce it to the world. Much that we attribute to God's will is not God's will at all, not according to the life Jesus lived and to the message that Jesus taught.

A man was visiting the Smithsonian in Washington taking pictures of some wax figures. He got to the one of Lady Bird Johnson, but there was a grandmother with her two granddaughters looking at it. He asked them if they would step aside momentarily so he could get a picture. They politely complied and the man took his picture, never noticing that he had asked the real Lady Bird Johnson (visiting the museum that day with her grandchildren) to move aside so he could take a picture of a wax model.

How often we are like that—seizing on a verse of Scripture here or there, applying values handed down by Grandpa, all the time failing to listen to the words of the Lord who came among us and died for us.

Never forget that the most perfect picture of God (Paul calls him "the image of the invisible God") is found by looking to Jesus Christ.

After the bombing of the marine headquarters in Beirut in 1983 the survivors were flown to the U.S. military hospital in West Germany. U. S. Marine Commander General Paul Kelly flew over from Washington to visit with the wounded and give them words of encouragement. He came to a certain marine who couldn't see and couldn't speak. So when he told him who he was, the marine reached up to the general's shoulders and felt the four stars that were there and knew this really was General Kelly.

We know, too, when we listen to the parables and look at the cross, when we see "sorrow and love flow mingled down"—we know that God has come to us, to do for us what we could never do for ourselves.

## IV.

So God reveals himself to us in nature, and reveals himself more fully in the Scriptures. But he reveals himself most perfectly in Jesus Christ. Yet there is a fourth way that we know about God, a fourth way that He reveals himself. He comes to us in our daily lives and shows himself time and time again if we will only look and listen for him.

C. S. Lewis gives an example in one of his essays that is just like the sort of thing we experience, too. He was planning a trip to London and was going to get a haircut before going. However, word came in the mail that he no longer needed to go to London. "Very well," he thought, "I won't have to get a haircut either." But something nagged at him anyway. And he couldn't get any peace until he decided to go ahead and get his hair cut. The barber was a friend of his, and when Lewis opened the door, the barber sighed and said, "I've been praying that you would come today. I need your help."

You may say "aha—coincidence" and you may be right. But you may also be wrong. A seminary professor told of a trip he and his family were taking, heading home for Christmas. The weather was bad and they hit a patch of ice in the road. The car skidded out of control, spun around several times, and came to a stop one foot from a power line pole. They all momentarily held their breaths. But there was more to it than that. There was an experience of God's presence. They had been delivered.

No, you couldn't prove it. But they felt it. I recall the beautiful lines from Tennyson:

> I found Him not in world or sun,
> Or eagle's wings, or insect's eye,
> Nor through the questions men may try,
> The petty cobwebs we have spun.
>
> If e'er when faith had fall'n asleep,
> I heard a voice "Believe no more;"
> And heard an ever-breaking shore
> That tumbled in the Godless deep,
>
> A warmth within the breast would melt
> The freezing reason's colder part,
> And like a man in wrath the heart
> Stood up and answered, "I have felt."

The wonder is not all in nature, wonderful as it is.

The truth is not all in Scripture, inspired as it is.

The full wonder and truth is in Jesus, the Christ, who came among us and died for us—and do not miss it—who stands today at our door and knocks.

# 5
# Great Beliefs of the Christian Faith:
## CREATION

*Genesis 1:1*

¹In the beginning God created the heavens and the earth.

*Psalm 90:1-2*

¹Lord, you have been our dwelling place throughout all generations. ²Before the mountains were born or you brought forth the earth and the world, from everlasting to everlasting you are God.

The doctrine of creation is not about the evolutionists versus the creationists. In fact, both of them are wrong. The evolutionist who thinks that the vast and complex world of nature is an accident and not the reflection of an omnipotent and personal God simply misses the picture. And the creationist who fails to see the evidence that God probably created over a long period of time, laboring as a potter would shape the clay, also misses the picture.

If we're going to be honest with the biblical text, we must admit that the biblical writers were far more interested in *who* than in *how*. Genesis doesn't tell us how God brought us into being, but there is no mistaking who did it. The Gospel writers don't tell us by what amazing chemistry or supernatural feat Jesus turned the water into wine, multiplied the fish and the loaves, walked on the sea, or brought the dead to life. But it is clear *who* did it.

So accepting the fact that creation is God's work, however he may have worked, we can move on to ask: But what does the doctrine of creation mean to me? What does it tell me? I believe we will find that it answers three important questions for each of us this morning: Who am I?, Where am I?, and Why am I?

Several years ago the television mini-series "Roots" created quite a sensation across the country. More people watched it than have watched any other series before or since. The series goes back to a book by the same name written by a man named Alex Haley, a black man who wanted to know more about where he came from. He traced his lineage back through slavery to Africa and to an ancestor named Kunta Kinte.

The idea behind "Roots" is not a new one. People have always wanted to know their past, hoping perhaps to find themselves related to a Washington, or a Jefferson, or a Lincoln, or a Rockefeller. I recall a time when I was 10-12 years old and we were discussing our family tree, picking up last names and maiden names back for only a couple of generations. Somewhere on my mother's side there popped up the last name "Jackson." My father jokingly said that we must be related to Andrew Jackson and Stonewall Jackson. Although he meant it as humor, I took it as gospel and knew from that moment that I would someday be President of the United States!

To some extent most of us are intrigued by our genealogies, but we are also frustrated because none of them go back far enough. We may trace our roots back to the late 1700s, but who were we going all the way back to when Jesus was born?

The same problem is true in the Bible, where the family tree is almost an obsession with the Jews. That's why the first nine chapters of Chronicles list name after name, going all the way back to Adam. Still it does not go far enough. Matthew's record of our Lord's family tree goes back to Abraham, which is not yet far enough. In fact there is only one genealogy that I know of that goes back far enough and that is in Luke, chapter 3, where the writer traces the ancestors of Jesus and ends up, not with Adam, but with God.

Now there is the end of the matter, or rather, its beginning. That is where the search for our roots must come to rest, where every family tree, every table of ancestors, and every genealogy must find itself to be complete. This is what is expressed in the very first sentence of the Bible, "In the beginning God created the heavens and the earth." There in the first chapters in the Bible, God teaches us three of the most important things we need to know about ourselves: Who we are, where we are, and why we are.

I.

First we learn who we are. Perhaps nothing is more pathetic than not knowing who you are. A pastor friend was telling me of his mother, who has had Alzheimer's disease for 15 years, and is still not old enough to receive social security. She has been in a nursing home, losing the use of her mind a little at a time. I asked my friend if his mother still knew him, her own son. "No," he replied, "she hasn't known anybody for years. She doesn't even know who she is."

Not long ago Reader's Digest carried the story of a man who had been reunited with his family after many years of separation. He had gone to take the bus one day and slipped on a patch of ice. He hit his head in the fall, lost his memory and had no idea who he was or where he was going. He got on the bus and where he got off nobody knew. Only years later did his memory come back so that he was able to be reunited with his family.

Both of these stories are tragic, but how tragic, too, that so much of the world lives as if to say the same thing: We don't know who we are. Genesis 1:1 teaches that we are God's creatures. "In the beginning *God created* . . . ." We have been made. The human race is not here because we willed it to be, but because God willed it. The creative force that peopled the planet is not humanity's; it is God's.

Have you ever heard a child ask a parent, "Was I an accident, or did you want me?" There is a tension in that question, and some days we want to direct it to our heavenly Father. Are we accidents that evolved one on top of the other until one cell became two and at the end of the line you have human beings? Or are we creatures created willfully, purposefully, carefully by a Heavenly Father? The teaching of our faith is straightforward. It tells us who we are by telling us whose we are: "In the beginning, God created . . . ."

II.

Now another thing this verse teaches us is *where* we are. You may think that doesn't matter, but I believe there is about us a kind of homing instinct. It is a truth played out in nature: we cannot rest until we know we are home.

Look at the birds that fly south and north, season after season, but always in some sense on their way home. Or consider the salmon that will not deposit her eggs until she swims upstream in what is truly a heroic attempt to get home again. I had an uncle who had a keen homing instinct. He used to say to his wife and nine children, when they were getting ready to go somewhere, "Let's hurry up and go so we can hurry up and get back."

There is about home a sense of belonging, of being in place. A few years ago some of my brothers, my Dad, and I drove just across the state line into North Carolina to see "the old home place." We walked in the front door, into the old front room, and Dad stopped. His eyes teared up, and pointing over to the corner, he said, "That's where my father died, lying on a bed right there." It was a sacred moment.

In tracing our roots, one of the questions we must ask is, Where is home? And the answer is in the Scriptures: "Lord, you have been our dwelling place throughout all generations. Before the mountains were born or you brought forth the earth and the world, from everlasting to everlasting, you are God." (Psalm 90:1-2).

You don't often catch that truth in literature, but Thornton Wilder's great play, "Our Town," is an exception. In the play a letter was addressed to someone. It had the name and street as usual, then continued "Grover's Corners, New Hampshire/U.S.A./ Western Hemisphere/Planet Earth/Milky Way/the Mind of God."

Now grasp that if you will. That is where we are. We are in God's world—not vagabonds or stowaways on a planet careening without purpose through a vast void. It is as Brunner said, "The world is in God." In the twentieth century the universe keeps getting bigger, or, rather, we keep seeing bigger pieces of it. But go as far as you can and God is farther. Discover as much as you can and God is more.

Who are we? We are God's creatures. Where are we? We're in God's world.

### III.

Finally, we ask, Why are we? It is a temptation at this point to become philosophical. That often happens when a question begins with why. But nothing could be plainer or simpler than the why of humankind. Why did God create us in the first place?

To answer that, let's ask another question: Why do you have children? Why do we put up with their self–centeredness, their disobedience, their constant demands? Why do we spend money on them, and save money for them? And why do so many couples who cannot have children themselves invest so much time and effort in adopting a child?

The answer, for the most part, is that our children are born out of our love, our *desire* to love, and our *need* to love. And it is a love that exceeds the disappointment and hurt that inevitably come with having children.

The Bible says that "God is love." And in that three–word sentence is the explanation behind us. Humanity was created out of the love of God. We are an expression of that love—of the desire for fellowship, of the wish to share in adventure, and of the hope which all parents nurture that we will be true to our roots. And it is a love that will stop at nothing—even to the point of dying on a cross for our sins.

I want to close with a story that I recall my pastor telling when I was growing up. It says so well what we need to hear in summary.

A little boy lived with his parents on a canal that was connected to the Mississippi River. He made him a little boat out of a block of wood, a couple of nails, and a little piece of cloth as a sail. He tied a string to it so he could watch the flow of water take it out aways, then pull it back into safety. Then he would tie the string to a tree to hold his boat safely overnight. One morning he went out to check on the boat and it was gone. The string, being so often in and out of the water, had broken and the boat had drifted away.

Several months later the boy and his father were shopping in the city downriver. They were walking down the sidewalks, looking in shop windows, when they happened to pass a junk shop. Something caught the boy's eye. He grabbed his Dad and they looked closer. Sure enough there was the boy's little boat thrown over to one side of a pile of junk. The boy went in and asked the proprietor how much he wanted for this boat. With a twinkle in his eye, he said, "For you, a nickel." The boy reached into his pocket and pulled out all that he had—one nickel. He gave it to the man, then took the boat and hugged it to his chest and said, "Little boat, you are twice mine now—once because I made you, and twice because I bought you."

# 6
# Great Beliefs of the Christian Faith:
## SIN—AT ODDS WITH OURSELVES

*Genesis 1:27*

[27]So God created man in his own image, in the image of God he created him; male and female he created them.

*Romans 3:23*

[23]For all have sinned and fall short of the glory of God.

*2 Corinthians 5:21*

[21]God made him who had no sin to be sin for us, so that in him we might become the righteousness of God.

Have you ever said or done something that was mean-spirited and then said to yourself afterwards, "That wasn't like me" or "That wasn't the real me?" It's as if there is a conflict or struggle going on inside between two of us—one wanting to do what's right, the other wanting to say or do what's small, or ugly, or hateful. You're not alone in that. Listen to what Paul says in one of his letters:

> My own behavior baffles me. I often find that I have the will to do good, but not the power. That is, I don't accomplish the good I set out to do, and the evil I don't really want to do I find that I am always doing. In my mind I'm God's willing servant, but in my own nature I am bound fast . . . to the law of sin and death. It is an agonizing situation . . . . (J. B. Phillips from Rom 7)

Why do we have this conflict? The answer goes all the way back to the creation account in the Book of Genesis. There in the very first chapter we find the reason for our dilemma: "Then God said; Let us make man in our image, in our likeness, and let them rule over the fish of the sea and the birds of the air, over the livestock, over all the earth, and over all the creatures that move along the ground. So God created man in his own image, in the image of God he created him; male and female he created them."

So far, so good. We have tremendous beginnings—each of us, because we are made in the image of God. Each of us, and everybody we know, and all the peoples of the world—all have something of the image of God about them. That's the upside of the story. The downside in this part of what it means to be made in the image of God is to have the freedom to make choices.

I.

From the beginning of the Bible to the end, we are creatures who are given by the Deity the right to choose which way we will live, how we will behave, what our priorities will be, and how we will treat each other. In Genesis, Adam is told not to eat of the tree of knowledge. But he has a choice. Will he eat or won't he? Why didn't God just build a fence around all these things we're not supposed to do? Because he made us in his image, and that means we may—we must—choose for ourselves. Does not Joshua say to the people, "Choose this day whom you will serve." And in the last book of the Bible we have the unforgettable picture of Jesus standing at the door knocking, waiting for a response. And you and I have a choice: We can open the door and invite him in, or we can choose not to open the door, not to respond to his presence.

I read a story this week about a young woman who is a track star. What is unusual about this young woman is not the fact that she runs track, but the astonishing truth that she is blind. How can a blind person even participate in such a sport, much less be a standout? The explanation lies in the fact that she wears a tiny radio receiver with a small speaker in her ear. Her coach sits in the stands and radios instructions to her: "Move to the left. There's someone on your right. You're coming to a curve." And because of his guidance, she can compete.

In a way we are like that. We are running the race and we, too, are blind. We don't know what's beyond the next curve. We don't always know the right thing to do. But God will guide us. There's a catch. We have a choice. The girl on the track has a choice, too. She can ignore the coach's guidance. And we can ignore God's.

So you see, the doctrine of sin begins on a good note. We are made in God's image. That means we are given sovereignty over the earth. Everything that was put here was put here for our joy and benefit. It means we are related to God—He has made us and wants to fellowship with us. It means that God has not left us to wander and wonder how we should live our lives. But it also means this: We have a choice. And in our choices we have distorted what we were intended to be, and have made a mockery of how we were intended to live.

## II.

The second thing to be said about sin is the often quoted verse from Paul: "All have sinned and come short of the glory of God." Sin is not just a problem for a few. It is a problem for everybody. It is not a question of which generation you belong to, how much education you have, which church you attend, or whether or not you even go to church. Sin is universal; it's everybody's problem. It isn't us against them. It's all of us, period.

Our younger son, Daniel, illustrated this point vividly one day not long ago. We were riding along in the car—just the two of us—when he asked, "Dad, did Jonathan mess in his pants when he was little?" Daniel had had an accident the night before so this was an important question for him. I assured him that his older brother had done just that, but he was not content to let the matter rest there. After a little delay he asked, "What about Mom? Did she mess in her pants when she was little?" I told him that although I wasn't there, I had no doubt that she, too, had messed in her pants. He paused a few moments, furrowed his brow and summoned his courage, and then asked meekly, "Dad, did you mess in your pants when you were little?" I said boldly (my reputation about to go out the window), "Yes, Daniel, even Dad messed in his pants when he was little." He let out a big sigh of relief and grinned with contentment as he made the (to him) startling discovery: So we all messed in our pants! Even children can grasp an idea of how widespread sin is. After all, they see it every day, too.

A day care worker relayed an experience from the playground that shows you something of what I mean. Three little children were playing in the sandbox, each with a toy can. Another child came up and sat on the edge of the sandbox, watching without saying anything. Soon one of the three said, "He's not playing with my can"; and the other two chimed in instantly, "mine neither."

Obviously such action is not to be equated with crimes of robbery or murder, but it points out what is at the heart of sin. It is to make the wrong choice, to choose self over God or neighbor. Jesus didn't really give us a complex code to follow. He gave us two rules and even they were not original. Both came from the Old Testament: "Love the Lord your God with all your heart, mind, and strength; and love your neighbor as yourself." All sin is in some way to do other than this.

Several years ago we had a hurricane to develop just off the eastern coast. It turned north and continued on a path past Georgia, South Carolina, and North Carolina. Its winds reached 135 mph, but the real danger lay in the fact that the National Hurricane Center could offer no prediction of where the storm might head next. The forecaster at the center said, "The problem this morning is we have a hurricane with no sense of direction." He went on to explain that there were no "steering currents" as there usually are; therefore, the storm could go anywhere.

That is something like our problem. We have lost our sense of direction. We were made to be in fellowship with God and with each other, but we have missed it.

In the fifteenth chapter of Luke, Jesus tells three parables that describe our situation as a kind of lostness. In the first parable he tells of a shepherd who had a hundred sheep. Ninety-nine of them were safe, but one was lost, and it was lost accidentally. The sheep never intended to be separated from the flock, but it had gone searching for grass to nibble, and ended up moving a little farther away, bit by little bit, until it was lost. Some of us are like that sheep. We never intended to nibble ourselves out of the way. We thought we were harmlessly doing what seemed natural. We said "one more time" or "just a little farther" or "it won't really matter" and before you knew it we were in trouble.

The second parable is about a woman sweeping out her house looking for a lost coin. Like the previous parable something is lost, but this time it's lost right at home. How this one hits us. We don't have to go across the sea to see sin; it's right here in our own homes—in children who do not honor their parents, in husbands who run around on their wives, in wives who gossip, in parents who fail to teach their children by their own example about the proper priorities and values of life.

The third parable Jesus tells in this chapter is the famous story of the prodigal son, who demands his inheritance and becomes lost in a far country. He squanders his wealth in riotous living and ends up in the pen with the pigs. This is "far country" sin. It is a metaphor for the worst of our sins. It is humanity at its ugliest and dirtiest—it is life at the bottom.

Do you see what has happened? We started out created in the image of a loving God. We end up distorting that image by wandering away a little at a time, or hurting those who love us most, or, worse, wallowing with pigs. We have lost more than our image or innocence or direction. We have lost our true selves.

One further word on the fact that all of us are caught up in sin. There are some who believe in sinless perfection, who believe it is possible to live a life without sin. Suppose you really were such a person; you still are tainted by sin because all of us are caught up in the sin of the system, what theologians call corporate sin, which is the sin of the way things work in the world.

Ron Sider illustrates this well: "Two hundred years ago in England, law–abiding, devoutly Christian mine owners regularly hired ten year old children to work in their mines. The children worked for ten to sixteen hours a day in low, muddy tunnels. The terrible conditions often led to sickness and death within a few years. The Christian mine–owner, meanwhile, made a handsome profit and sent his sons to Oxford or Cambridge. At about the same period, slave ships carried Africans to North America, where they became property to be bred and worked like animals."

You may reply that *you* never worked children in a mine or traded in slaves, but we are caught up in a system that is just as sinful. We Americans use a greater percentage of the world's resources than is justified by our population. We drive our cars, heat and cool our homes, our office, and in so many of our choices show little regard for our less fortunate brothers and sisters in other places. We fought a war in the Persian Gulf because there was oil under the ground. We refused to get involved in Yugoslavia, where thousands have been killed and millions are refugees. We refused until it was almost too late to get involved in Somalia, where starvation is rampant because armed bandits steal the food.

You and I didn't make these choices consciously or directly, but we are caught up in them because we are part of the system. Paul knew what he was saying, "*All* have sinned . . ." and nothing has happened since to qualify that in any way. It is as true today as when it was written 1900 years ago.


III.


So much for the source and the dimensions of the problem. Finally, we must ask, "What can we do about it?" And the answer is that God has already done something about it and the solution is ours for the asking. Paul writes in II Corinthians 5, "God made him who had no sin to be sin for us so that we might attain to the righteousness of God." Do you see that we have come full circle? We began with the image of God, which sin has distorted and in some cases all but covered up; and we end up having come full circle back to the righteousness of God. We can, however, like the prodigal son come back home to who we really are, because God has provided a way. And the way is at once both simple and profound. The problem is sin and the solution is Jesus, his death on the cross to pay the penalty for our sins.

During the Second World War an American paratrooper was dropped behind enemy lines in rural France. He landed in a field with only one farmhouse in sight. He went quickly to that farmhouse where an older French couple took him in and hid him. Two Germans, however, saw the parachute come down and knew that there was only one farmhouse in the area where the paratrooper could have hidden. They searched and found him, but instead of executing him first, they took the older gentleman outside and shot him for collaborating with the enemy. In all the confusion the American paratrooper fled into the woods. When the two Germans went to get help to track him down, he backtracked and came back to the little farmhouse, where the weeping Frenchwoman opened the door. He explained that they would never expect to find him there again, so she took him in one more time to hide him. The Germans returned with re–enforcements and searched for days in the nearby woods, but never found the American paratrooper. They never thought to check the house again.

Sometimes the thing we are searching for is where we'd least expect it and nearer than we ever thought. Who would ever have looked to a small hill outside Jerusalem to find God's way of forgiving our sins?

But there it is for all who will see it, and believe it, and accept it. There it is for those whose sin is accidental, who never really intended to do any wrong. There it is for broken homes and broken relationships. There it is, even for sins committed in the "far country" when we acted more like animals than human beings made in God's image.

Whatever you may be dealing with today that needs to be resolved, whatever accounts need to be settled, whatever wrongs need to be made right—get on with it, and come home to the cross, where God in his own way has made provision for the sin problem and says, "You are forgiven."

# 7
# Great Beliefs of the Christian Faith:
# THE ATONEMENT

*Mark 10:45*

[45]For even the Son of Man did not come to be served, but to serve, and to give his life as a ransom for many.

*Colossians 1:13*

[13]For he has rescued us from the dominion of darkness and brought us into the kingdom of the Son he loves.

*Hebrews 2:17*

[17]For this reason he had to be made like his brothers in every way, in order that he might become a merciful and faithful high priest in service to God, and that he might make atonement for the sins of the people.

*Romans 3:25*

[25]God presented him as a sacrifice of atonement, through faith in his blood. He did this to demonstrate his justice, because in his forbearance he had left the sins committed beforehand unpunished.

*Romans 5:6-8*

[6]You see, at just the right time, when we were still powerless, Christ died for the ungodly. [7]Very rarely will anyone die for a righteous man, though for a good man someone might possibly dare to die. [8]But God demonstrates his own love for us in this: While we were still sinners, Christ died for us.

The last sermon dealt with sin, first with its origin: We are made in God's image, which means among other things that we have choices, and we invariably choose not to put God and neighbor first, but to put ourselves first. Then we spoke of sin's dimension: "All have sinned." The problem is not only out there, it is also in here. Finally, we looked at God's solution for sin: God came in the flesh in Jesus Christ who died on the cross for our sins, and who arose from the dead on the third day.

What we want to focus on today is God's solution for sin, and particularly the part, "died on the cross for our sins." How did Jesus' death on a cross in ancient Palestine take care of our sins? And why did he do it in such a way?

Those are the questions we will be looking at this morning as we consider the Atonement. The word atonement means that some wrong has been made right, or more specifically that a broken relationship has been re-established. You can see what it means by dividing the word up: at–one–ment. God has taken measures to make sinners at–one with him.

Sometimes when we set out to understand something we have to unlearn some things that we may have assumed or thought correct in order to learn the way to a better understanding. The Doctrine of the Atonement is one of those cases where we need to begin by unlearning some faulty ideas and then take another look at the Scriptures to see what the proper understanding is.

I read where one pastor was trying to explain the atonement to children. He took a dirty glass with dirty water in it and said, "This represents the sin of your life, all the filthiness, all the lies, all the wrong deeds." Then he showed a hammer and said, "This represents God's justice." Then he proceeded to put the dirty glass of water on a table and to raise his hammer to smash it to pieces, explaining that God can not tolerate sin. The hammer came down in a tremendous blow and just before it smashed the glass to smithereens, the preacher slipped a pan between the glass and the hammer, so that when the hammer hit, it made a loud thud and left a dent in the pan. The pan, he explained, was Jesus, who took the blow that we should have received.

In some ways he was making the point, but the children, instead of feeling a sigh of relief that their sin could be forgiven, were frightened at the idea of God as a hammer just waiting to pulverize them. This is the problem with many presentations of the Atonement—God comes off looking more like an evil dictator than a loving Father.

Another distorted view of the Atonement goes back hundreds of years. It's known as the fish hook theory and goes something like this: Jesus was used as the bait to catch the Devil. The devil took the bait and it looked like he had won when Jesus died; but the Devil lost three days later when Jesus arose from the dead. Somehow it seems unbefitting the glory and holiness of a righteous God to think of him playing fishing games with the Devil.

One final idea about the Atonement that needs to be unlearned, or at least put in its proper perspective, is the idea of a substitutionary atonement, the idea that Jesus died for sins as a substitute for those of us who deserved punishment for our sins. The reason we need to reconsider it is *not* because it isn't true, but because it isn't the whole picture.

So what is the bigger picture of the Atonement? What does it mean to say that Jesus died on the cross for our sins? This is what I want to make clear this morning: (1) that the New Testament speaks of the Atonement in a variety of images—at least four, maybe more, but certainly more than the one that is so often singled out; (2) that the Atonement is an expression of God's love on our behalf; and (3) that the Atonement was costly.

I.

First, the New Testament uses a variety of images to tell us what Jesus's death on the cross means.

(a) One image is taken from *the slave market*, where the people have lost their freedom and are being sold into slavery. Slavery was very common in biblical times, with conquering armies often carrying off whole populations. In this image someone steps up and pays a ransom for the slaves. He purchases freedom for people who cannot free themselves. Jesus says, in Mark 10:45, "For even the Son of Man did not come to be served, but to serve, and to give his life as a ransom for many." This is the kind of imagery Paul had in mind when he wrote, "You are not your own, you were bought with a price."

(b) Another image comes from *the battlefield*. On Good Friday Jesus gave his life in the fight to free humanity from sin, and it looked at the end of the day as if he had lost the battle. But on Easter Sunday he arose victorious and the battle was won. Paul had this imagery in mind when he wrote in the first chapter of Colossians, "For he has rescued us from the dominion of darkness and brought us into the kingdom of the Son he loves, in whom we have redemption, the forgiveness of sins." This is also the image in a popular religious song: "It is finished. The battle is over."

(c) A third image for the Atonement comes from *the Temple's altar* where the priest sacrifices animals. Blood is shed to atone for the people's sins. In the New Testament Jesus is both priest and sacrifice. The writer of Hebrews puts it this way: "He (Jesus) had to be made like his brothers in every way in order that he might become a merciful and faithful high priest in service to God, and that he might make atonement for the sins of the people" (Hebrews 2:17-18). Paul rounds out the picture when he writes in Romans, "God presented him as a sacrifice of atonement, through faith in his blood."

(d) In another image for the Atonement the setting is a *courtroom*. God is the judge and before him stand people who are guilty. But one who is righteous and free takes the sentence of the people upon himself and dies in their place. Paul puts it this way in Romans 5:6, 8: "You see, at just the right time, when we were powerless, Christ died for the ungodly. God demonstrates his own love for us in this: While we were still sinners, Christ died for us."

So you see the Bible speaks of the Atonement in a number of ways. Just as Jesus made the same point with different parables, so the New Testament writers try to convey the meaning of Jesus's death on the cross in a variety of ways, from the slave market to the battlefield, to the altar, to the courtroom. All of them are part of the picture, but not one of them captures the whole story or the full meaning of what happened at Calvary.

## II.

The Atonement is an expression of God's love on our behalf. Paul writes in II Corinthians 5:19, "God was reconciling the world to himself in Christ, not counting men's sins against them."

Sometimes people look at the cross almost as if it were an act of revenge instead of an act of love, as if God were angry and Jesus had to appease him. But this is not true. God and humanity were separated by sin, but it was God, not us, who took the initiative to fix the situation. Recall the subject of the verse we just read, "*God* was reconciling the world." "The world," as the old Christmas carol goes, "in solemn slumber lay."

One of the great truths of the Christian faith is that God is the great seeker. God comes looking for us long before we reach out to him. And he comes looking not to back us up, not to give us our just desserts, but to extend the hand of friendship which includes both fellowship and forgiveness if we will but take it.

The great English preacher Charles Spurgeon used to tell about a poor woman who had trouble paying her rent. The deacons took up a collection to pay her rent and sent a deacon with the money. He went to her house, knocked on the door, waited, knocked again. There was no answer. Sunday he saw her in church and asked her why she didn't answer the door. She replied, "I thought you were the landlord coming to collect the rent." How often we think that the God who comes to save us is somehow out to get us.

I read an account recently about the famous opera singer Marian Anderson. In a small Nebraska college town she had given a concert that was the high point of the winter.

After the concert, she returned to the hotel and went up to the hotel desk. She asked the young woman behind the desk if she had attended the concert. The girl, a student working her way through college, explained how her job had kept her from attending the concert and how disappointed she was that she hadn't been able to hear the great singer. Then followed an unforgettable moment. There in the middle of the hotel lobby, with no accompaniment, Marion Anderson sang for the young college student the "Ave Maria."

The student couldn't come to the concert, so the concert, in a sense, came to the student. Calvary, for all its pain and horror, is God's concert for sinners. It was done out of love; it was done for our benefit. And it was done because God was willing to come among us in the flesh and to die for us on the cross. It was God's way. You remember Jesus saying, "You do not take my life from me. I give my life for you."

## III.

Which brings us to our final point: Atonement is costly. You've heard it said, "God's grace is free, but it's not cheap." The Atonement came at great cost, as we have known since that first memory verse that many of us learned: "For God so loved the world that he gave his only begotten son that whosoever believeth in him should not perish, but have everlasting life."

Back in the 1860s the nation was pushing to complete its first transcontinental railroad. One company was laboring from the west inland, the other was building from the plains toward the Rocky Mountains. The two finally joined up on May 10, 1869, at Promontory Point in Utah. There Governor Leland Stanford took a silver plated sledge hammer and drove a golden spike to complete the construction. One word went out over Western Union telegraph lines to announce the event, the word "done." It had been costly; many had lost their lives from the time the project began until it was finished. But finally it was done.

So it is with the Atonement. The spikes have been driven. Jesus gave his life and in his last words he announced, "It is finished." But look at the cost: "For God so loved the world that he gave his only Son."

Sometimes there's one nagging question that remains after the Atonement has been discussed or presented. That question is, Why did God do it this way? If God wanted to make peace with us, if he wanted to forgive us, why didn't he just say, "You're forgiven"?

There are, I believe, two reasons for that. First, forgiveness that costs nothing is worth nothing, or very little anyway. This is not a great theological insight, it's true in everyday life. Suppose, horror of horrors, that someone kidnapped and then killed a child of yours. What would you do—offer blanket forgiveness? Would you say, "No big deal. We're Christians; you're forgiven"? I don't think so. That wouldn't be a good demonstration of Christian forgiveness. It would seem to say to me that you didn't care much in the first place.

Do you recall the 1988 presidential election? One of the debates really hurt Michael Dukakis. The moderator asked what his reaction would be, as far as capital punishment were concerned, if someone raped his wife, Kitty. Dukakis never showed any emotion at all. He spoke as dispassionately as you could ever imagine—no sign of rage. And it cost him because even the commentators were repulsed at the idea of cheap grace.

God didn't offer any cheap grace; he offered his only Son to die on a cross.

There's another reason He did it this way. A pastor's grandson was in four–year–old kindergarten. Each week the children learned a memory verse. The pastor wanted to give the grandson a chance to shine at the worship service, so he asked him if he would repeat his memory verse for the congregation. He did. It was Genesis 9:13, "I do set my bow in the cloud." Realizing that the verse was a little unusual as a memory verse, the pastor followed up with a question, "And why did he set his bow in the cloud?" to which the boy responded with innocence and wisdom, "He just did it."

# 8
# Great Beliefs of the Christian Faith:
# SALVATION IN THREE TENSES

*Matthew 1:21*

²¹She will give birth to a son, and you are to give him the name Jesus, because he will save his people from their sins.

*Ephesians 2:8-10*

⁸For it is by grace you have been saved, through faith--and this not from yourselves, it is the gift of God—⁹not by works, so that no one can boast. ¹⁰For we are God's workmanship, created in Christ Jesus to do good works, which God prepared in advance for us to do.

*Colossians 1:13-14*

¹³For he has rescued us from the dominion of darkness and brought us into the kingdom of the Son he loves, ¹⁴in whom we have redemption, the forgiveness of sins.

*1 Corinthians 1:18*

¹⁸For the message of the cross is foolishness to those who are perishing, but to us who are being saved it is the power of God.

*Romans 5:9*

⁹Since we have now been justified by his blood, how much more shall we be saved from God's wrath through him!

Have you ever walked up to a stranger and asked, "Are you saved?" I doubt that many of us take that approach to sharing our faith. It is not hard to imagine some of the stares and remarks that you would receive. One might say, "I didn't know I was lost." Another might ask, "Saved from what?"

There would be good reason for misunderstanding because you and the other person would not be speaking the same language. You and I use words and phrases almost everyday that people outside the church simply do not understand. We speak in terms of sin, which most of the world probably equates with being naughty. We speak of "accepting Jesus as your Lord and Savior," of "making a profession of faith." You and I know what we mean by those things, but those outside the church are not converted when they hear them. They are more likely confused.

What I have been attempting in these sermons on the great beliefs is to speak of our faith in a way that allows people both within *and* outside the church to understand better, to grasp what it is that we as Christians believe.

The word "salvation" means liberation or release or deliverance. We use the word "saved" in our everyday lives the way the biblical writers use it. The student who was going to be called on next by the teacher had not prepared for class, but he was "saved by the bell." He was delivered from embarrassment. You may have heard one of the news commentators the past few days speaking of "saving the Somalians," which means, of course, that they have been delivered from starvation.

When the biblical writers speak of being saved, they, too, mean that we are delivered. And they speak of this salvation, or deliverance, in three tenses. They speak in the past tense, of something God has done that demands a response. They speak in the present tense, of something God is doing in our lives. And they speak in the future tense, of something God will complete on the day of judgment.

I.

First, salvation refers to something God has done that demands a response. What has God done? Paul puts it this way in Colossians

1:13-14: "He has rescued us from the dominion of darkness and brought us into the kingdom of the Son he loves, in whom we have redemption, forgiveness of sins."

An English theologian (R. E. O. White) explains that we are saved from "sin and death; guilt and estrangement; ignorance of truth; bondage to habit and vice; fear of demons, of death, of life, of God, of hell; despair of self; alienation from others; pressures of the world; a meaningless life."

There is a commonly known story that comes from the life of Martin Luther. The Devil approached him one day and tried to discourage him with the charge that all people, including Martin Luther, were fallible. To prove his point, he presented the reformer with a long list of sins of which he was guilty. To which Luther said, "Think a little harder and you can come up with some more." This the Devil did. Finally Luther told him, "Now write across all these sins in red ink, 'The blood of Jesus Christ, His Son, cleanses us from all sin.'"

That is what God has done. He has come in the flesh in Jesus Christ, who died for our sins, and rose again on the third day. But recall that salvation is something God has done that demands a response. What we do with God's offer of salvation, with his willingness to deliver us from sin and fear and meaningless, what we do is our decision, not God's.

Augustine said it well, "The God who made you without you will not save you without you." Salvation is not something God did *to* us; it is something he did *for* us and *with* us. It is God's offer of grace, but like anything else that is offered to you, you must accept it or reject it.

Before we go on to another tense of salvation, let's deal with the fact that many people question their salvation. They think that because their experience of deliverance was not like Paul's, because they had no Damascus Road experience, then they may not be saved. But listen: everybody's salvation experience is not the same. Some people do have dramatic conversions, but most people come into the faith like spring comes into season—gradually, perhaps slowly, with fits and starts. It isn't important how you become aware of God's grace. What matters most is that you respond to it.

Shakespeare put the matter in memorable words in *Julius Caesar*:

> There is a tide in the affairs of men,
> Which, taken at the flood,
>     leads on to fortune;
> Omitted, all the voyage of their life
> Is bound in shallows and in miseries.

## II.

So salvation refers first to something God has done for us, and to our response. Second, salvation refers to something God is doing in our lives. That is the present tense of salvation. Paul puts it this way in 1 Corinthians 1:18—"For the message of the cross is foolishness to those who are perishing, but to us who are being saved, it is the power of God."

Most of us refer to salvation in only the past tense: I was saved. But Paul understands it to be something that is still going on. It is a process of growth. It is the recognition of what the sign says, "Be patient. God isn't finished with me yet."

God isn't finished with any of us. Once we are saved, we are to grow in that salvation, to grow in grace.

Some of you remember when Frank Howard was the football coach at Clemson. One week his first and second string quarterbacks were injured in a game so he began practice the next week with the third and fourth string quarterbacks. On Monday of practice the third string quarterback was hurt; on Tuesday the fourth string quarterback was hurt; on Wednesday Coach Howard called the fifth string quarterback over to where he was standing. He looked at him, opened his hand, and said, "Poof. Son, you are now a first–string quarterback."

Now Frank Howard knew different, because he knew that you grow into a first string quarterback, that it comes only after hard work, preparation, and lots of practice.

The same is true of us on our spiritual pilgrimages. How often people feel frustrated and say, "Why can't I be like Mrs. So–and–So, or Deacon So–and–So?" Well, they weren't born that way. They have been reborn, but just as important, they have grown in grace. They have allowed God not only to save them, but to teach them and lead them.

I read a story recently of an atheist barber whose good friend was a Christian. They debated the faith back and forth with mutual respect. One day they were riding together through the slums of the big city where they lived. The atheist barber thought this a good opportunity to make a point. Turning to his friend, he asked, "If there really is a God why does he permit people to live such violent lives and to spend their days half drunk?"

At about that time a disheveled man crossed the street in front of them—his beard in need of trimming and his hair long and stringy. The friend seized the moment to respond to the atheist barber: "Why do you as a barber permit people to walk the streets so badly in need of a shave and a haircut?" The barber answered, "Well, he never gave me a chance to fix him up."

Isn't that true of some of us? We haven't given God the chance to make many improvements. We were saved on such–and–such a date, case closed. Only God didn't want to close the case there. He wanted to continue to work on us. There is plenty of need. People whose salvation is assured still speak words of hatred, intolerance, and prejudice. People converted years ago have never become the servants that Jesus called us to be. People who surrendered their lives in a tender moment surrendered only a portion, and held tightly to the rest lest God really make something new of them.

But there is no biblical warrant for that kind of salvation. God has begun a good work, but how he longs to bring it to perfection—if we would just let him.

### III.

There is a third way that salvation is spoken of in the Scriptures. It is in the future tense. Paul says in Romans 5:9—"Since we have now been justified by his blood, how much more *shall we be saved* from God's wrath through him!"

This refers to something that is going to happen. It refers to the deliverance that we shall experience on Judgment Day. What an uncomfortable thought is the idea of judgment. But it is inescapable. The Scriptures make it clear: "It is appointed once to die, and after that the judgment." And what do we have to offer on our own behalf as we stand with our lives an open book to hear sentence passed? What shall we say for ourselves—that we didn't know better? Most all of us know better. We know what it is God wants of us, and we know how far short of the mark we come. It isn't our knowing that's a problem; it's our doing.

How can we deal with judgment? The answer is clear for those who follow Jesus: We *shall* be saved. The great English preacher Charles Spurgeon once said that he was so sure of it that he could grab a cornstalk and swing out over the fires of hell, look the Devil in the face and sing, "Blessed Assurance, Jesus is mine."

Let me close with a parable I came across this week. A certain man decided that he would swim from Los Angeles to Hawaii. He spent years preparing, working out with the best coaches to be had anywhere. Finally the day came and he walked out into the ocean and began to swim in the vast Pacific Ocean, aiming for Hawaii.

He swam out farther and farther, 5, 10, 15 miles. At about 20 miles he realized that he would never be able to swim all the way to Hawaii; it was just too far. Just then a motorboat came by. With his last ounce of energy the swimmer called out, "Save me, please save me." The owner of the boat looked down at the drowning swimmer and said, "Friend, you're in trouble. What you need is the waterproof edition of my book on swimming to Hawaii. It will tell you everything you need to know. Here, catch it."

Then the motorboat pulled off and left the drowning seaman no better off. But, not to fear—another motor boat came by. Again the swimmer called out, "Save me! Please save me!" The owner looked down and said, "Friend, you're in trouble. What you need is someone to show you how to swim." With that the owner jumped into the water and demonstrated the Australian crawl, admonishing the swimmer just to follow his example and everything would be all right. Then he got back into his boat and pulled away.

The situation for the swimmer seemed hopeless until a third motorboat came by. Again the swimmer cried out, "Save me! Please save me." The owner looked over the edge of the boat and said, "Friend, you're in trouble. Worse than that, you're drowning." The owner reached out to the swimmer and pulled him out of the water, sat him in a chair, and gave him something to eat and something to drink. When he finished, the owner said, "You know we're only a couple hundred miles from Hawaii now, so you need to get back into the water and swim the rest of the way."

So the swimmer got back into the water, swam a few miles and found himself in the same situation he had been in before, gasping for breath and about to go under. About that time the fourth motorboat came by. The owner leaned over the side and said, "Friend, you're in trouble. Even worse, you're drowning! What you need is somebody to save you." And with that he reached out and pulled the swimmer on board. He fed him and gave him something to drink. Then he told him to sit back and rest until several hours later they docked and the boat captain delivered the swimmer to the golden sands of Hawaii.

Now which of these truly saved the drowning man? Of course it was the last motorboat captain, who not only pulled him out of the water, but also safely delivered him to his destination.

That is salvation—not a book of instructions, not a good example, not temporary help—but the assurance that God who came in Christ to die for our sins, continues to lead us in our pilgrimage, and promises to deliver us in the end. That is his gift, his offer to us. Whether we accept or not is, of course, left up to us.

# 9

# Great Beliefs of the Christian Faith:
## WHEN WE SAY CHURCH

*1 Corinthians 12:27-28*

²⁷Now you are the body of Christ, and each one of you is a part of it. ²⁸And in the church God has appointed first of all apostles, second prophets, third teachers, then workers of miracles, also those having gifts of healing, those able to help others, those speaking in different kinds of tongues.

*1 Corinthians 13:12*

¹²Now we see but a poor reflection as in a mirror; then we shall see face to face. Now I know in part; then I shall know fully, even as I am fully known.

People use the word "church" to mean a number of things. Some think of the church as a building, some think of a local congregation, and some think of the Christians around the world as the church. What should we mean when we say church?

## I.

First, and perhaps most naturally, people do think of a building when they say church. Point to any building with a steeple and stained glass windows and ask a child, "What is that?", and he or she will most certainly say, "That's a church." Later we usually try to reverse that thinking by teaching them that a church is not a building, but perhaps we shouldn't move too quickly beyond the fact that buildings, or designated places of worship, have always played a large role in the life of God's people.

In the Old Testament, even while the people were wandering

through the wilderness, they set up a Tent of Meeting, a kind of portable holy place. This was the ancestor, if you will, of the later temples in Jerusalem, the synagogues of the scattered Jews, and the houses of worship for the Christian community. There has always been an impulse among believers to set aside a place for worship. Sometimes these places have been on a grand scale, such as the cathedrals of Europe, and sometimes of very humble dimensions, such as the adobe huts that African converts have built. But whatever the building, it was set aside by the people as a special place, a place of worship, a place where people would come in the hopes of meeting with God.

I confess that I used to be one who thought all these church buildings were a waste of good resources. Imagine how difficult it must have been to build one of these great medieval cathedrals. There is almost no way to calculate in contemporary terms what one cost as generation after generation sacrificed, labored, and died—each making its contribution in turn. All this, I used to think, could have been given to these poor peasants and artisans to make their lives better instead of being squandered on a building. Thus did I think, until the first time I stepped into one, and felt the large silence, raised my eyes heavenwards to follow the climb of the arches, stood mute before the incredible stained glass windows that brought to artistic expression the story of our Lord, or of his parables, or of the people around him.

To walk into such a place is to discover: These people knew what they were doing. They weren't depriving the poor. They were enriching the life of every pauper and pilgrim who would ever enter to worship. They were erecting testimonies, not buildings. They were saying for all who would come later: What a great God we serve. We have done our best to create a place where people might sense something of his majesty and wonder.

And do you not think the people who sacrificed to build this sanctuary felt something of that same desire to honor God with the best they could do, and with something that through the ages would be a reminder of their faith and their willingness to sacrifice.

This is not a building, it's a testimony. And the steeple spires that dot this community and appear even in the country on the crest of a hill, or in the edge of the woods—erected by people long since departed—they, too, are testimonies to the yearning of the human spirit to experience the holy, to be forgiven of sin, to find refuge in the common ground of the faith.

But, the skeptic may say, doesn't the Bible clearly state that God doesn't dwell in structures made by human hands? Indeed the Bible does say that, and it's true. God is no more present in this sanctuary than he is in the empty high school gymnasium or in the restaurant down the street. The difference in our setting aside our buildings is not to help God be present with us; it is to help us be present with God. We come here to listen for the Word of God. We come here hoping and expecting. And this building says to those who pass by, here people gather to worship, to praise, to proclaim, to confess, to learn, to struggle, and to listen. The buildings are the church not because of what they mean to God, but because of what they mean to us as we seek to know God and to express our love for God.

II.

The second thing we mean when we say "church" is the body of believers, people here and around the world who are different from others not necessarily because we believe in God, (Many people believe in some kind of god.) but because we believe that God has revealed himself in Jesus Christ, who died on the cross for our sins and arose again on the third day. Our beliefs set us apart because our beliefs determine how we live.

Those beliefs known as the Ten Commandments are the very foundation of our civilization, and when they are flaunted, civilization begins to disintegrate. There was a story last week on "CBS' 60 Minutes" that proves the point. It was about a private school called the Piney Woods School. Unlike other schools, however, this one was not a refuge for those who did not want to deal with the woes of the inner city. Rather it was a refuge for kids *from* the inner city. All of them were black; all came out of neighborhoods ravaged by violence, drug abuse, and a general breakdown in community.

In the Piney Woods School, headed by a black man with deep convictions and great commitment, these students were taught difficult high school subjects and excelled. What made the difference in their lives? Two things: order, and love. Order, meaning rules, restrictions, and responsibilities—every student had to work ten hours per week, usually doing work that we would call common labor—order that was not voted on, but was enforced, order that meant a school uniform instead of competitive fashions that cost badly needed money, order that meant no television and tolerated no violence, order that meant (can you imagine!) prayer services three times a day. And love: genuine caring from teachers and those in authority. The result is that 90 percent of the student body that only a few years before might have been headed for prison are now headed for college.

A miracle you say? Wrong! The same kind of environment will do the same thing for the students coming in as it did for the students graduating out. It is an old principle—relying on the order God provided and expressing the love God intended.

The church is different from other institutions today because it is the only place I know of where that message is being preached, and where the people are trying to live it out. We believe that it does matter what you believe and how you behave.

Some will immediately jump back and say, as someone almost invariably does, "Well, those Christians down there at First Baptist (or any other church) are a bunch of hypocrites. They do things all week that are wrong and then gather on Sunday as a bunch of saints." Well, that is true. We haven't gotten our lives up to our ideals yet. That's one reason we have to keep coming back—to be reminded again and again of just what it is God expects of us. But the fact that we come means we're working on it. It means we agree with Augustine, "Our hearts are restless, Lord, until they rest in thee." But it also means that we know our sins and that we know we haven't arrived at perfection. We gather, not so much because we believe ourselves to be saints (as the term is commonly used), but because we know ourselves to be sinners, and because we believe in forgiveness.

What binds us together with Christians around the world is that we are striving to follow the same Lord and to become by his grace the people of God.

III.

So the church is a building, and a body of believers. Third, it is the body of Christ. We could spend a great deal of time discussing what Paul meant by that phrase, but in its simplest and most straightforward sense it means that the work of the church in the world is to do the work of Christ. It is to preach and to teach, to help those in need, to work for justice, to comfort those who are suffering—to do the kinds of things Jesus was about when he walked the earth. In short, to be a part of the church is to report for duty in God's army, where everything that you do in God's name matters.

I read this week of a cattle ranch out West that still works as a ranch, where people come to learn and to do what cowboys did a hundred years ago. One of the first things they do as the day begins is bring the horses up and line them up for the modern cowboys to pick a mount for the day. The interesting thing is how the horses line up. Without any coaching they assemble themselves in a row, standing shoulder to shoulder, often even lining up in the same spot. Not all of them are picked every day. Some get picked; some get sent back to await another day. I think it is much like that with us. It is not whether we get picked for the foreign mission field or for the pastorate, to teach adults or to keep the nursery, to be deacon or to change diapers. What matters is that we report for duty, and in doing so remember the closing lines of Milton's famous sonnet, "They also serve who only stand and wait."

In 1939 Baker James Cauthen was one of the best known and respected Baptist preachers. He pastored a large church in Fort Worth and taught at Southwestern Seminary. Although he and his wife had two small children, and though war was raging in many places, nonetheless the Cauthens felt it God's will that they go abroad as missionaries. Many people made a great deal of their decision and it was even remarked at their appointment, "Boy, we caught a big fish this time, didn't we?" But Cauthen never saw it that way, and neither I think did God. For Cauthen it was a matter of reporting for duty and then of doing God's will. He said that if he died on a ship that was bombed in Hong Kong harbor, it would be all right because he knew they were in God's will.

If we were to write the story of the life of the church, one of the most inspiring chapters would tell how the world has been changed by ordinary people like you and me who reported for duty, who offered their lives, talents, and fortunes in service to God and with no strings attached. The number of such is legion. But we must be honest in seeing the other side, too. What could yet be accomplished in the name of Christ if all the people sitting in the pews reported for duty? What kind of ministry is going undone because there is no one to do it, or to organize it, or to pay for it?

I read the story several years ago of a church in Eastern Europe. An American soldier had seen it during his time of service and wanted after the war to bring his wife back to see the village church that had so impressed him. What he found, however, was a small pile of stones. A citizen of the town explained that the members had taken the church apart to use the stones on their farms and in the village. "I guess," he said, "that's all it was useful for anymore."

## IV.

The church is a building that represents our hopes and our needs. It is, second, believers who share in common a commitment to Jesus Christ. It is, third, the body of Christ—believers seeking God's will and doing God's work in the world.

Finally, the church is a beginning, not an end. It is not people who have arrived, but people who are traveling toward a common destination. It is as if every service ends with the words broadcast after each segment of a television mini-series, "To be continued."

One of the great sermons of the 20$^{th}$ century was preached by the English apologist C. S. Lewis and was entitled, "The Weight of Glory." In closing, Lewis pointed out that the weight of glory is the recognition that those souls with whom we worship and fellowship will one day be with us, or us with them, in heaven where things are recognized for what they really are. So that the most humble soul here, whose faithfulness is never noted, but whose work has been done day after day, will be honored there for shaping the world against the same kind of overwhelming odds that a stream of water would face if called upon to cause a chasm like the Grand Canyon. Yet she works on, unheralded and often unobserved. In heaven she will be known for the saint she is. The weight of glory is not only that we shall know, but, as Paul so clearly says, that we shall be known.

I've just finished reading a novel called *Jewel*, the name of the woman who is the chief character in the story. She and her family grew up in Mississippi, but after some considerable persuading, she gets her husband to move to California. The year is 1952.

One of the differences between life in Mississippi and life in California is illustrated by an incident that occurs soon after she moves. She is going to visit an office where she hopes to get help for her retarded daughter. The only available parking space requires her to parallel park. As she tries to do so, a young black boy—perhaps 7 or 8 years old—is walking down the sidewalk on the way to school. He sees the lady who is trying to parallel park, stops where he is, and directs her into the space, then with a wave of the hand, continues on to school.

In all her life, Jewel has never experienced a neatly dressed black child walking to school in a white neighborhood. Then she gets out of the car and meets a black lady pushing her baby in a stroller. So it isn't a white neighborhood after all. Then she goes into the foundation office, which is really a beautiful old house that has been converted, and she meets a black secretary. By this time she is almost speechless because she realizes in a way she never has before that the world is partly black.

Now there's one more surprise waiting, but it isn't in the novel.

It is a surprise waiting for each of us, and that is that not only is the world partly black, but so is heaven—populated by souls who are there not because of their color, but like all of us, in spite of our sins. They will be those who sang in the fields, and served in the homes, and lived their lives largely in a combination of both fear and faith. They will be there, where we finally know, but also where we are finally known.

The weight of glory, the church's glory, is that it does matter how we treat those around us. We have been commanded not only to love God, but to love our neighbors as well—as well, in fact, as we love ourselves. What kind of hope then do we have? We are all tainted, whatever our color, with words that have hurt, thoughts that have corrupted, and deeds that have belied our being the people of God. How in the world can *we* be the church?

Well this is not, after all, the end; it is the beginning. We are not what we ought to be, but at least we have a good idea of what we ought to be.

Let me close with one of my favorite passages from the German monk, Martin Luther:

> This life therefore is not righteousness
> but growth in righteousness
> not health but healing,
> not being but becoming
> not rest but exercise.
>
> We are not yet what we shall be
>  but we are growing toward it,
>  the process is not yet finished
>  but it is going on,
>  this is not the end,
>  but it is the road.
>
> All does not yet gleam in glory
> but all is being purified.

# 10
# Great Beliefs of the Christian Faith:
## WORSHIP—THE 3 R'S OF WORSHIP

*Psalm 24*

[1]The earth is the Lord's, and everything in it, the world, and all who live in it; [2]for he founded it upon the seas and established it upon the waters. [3]Who may ascend the hill of the Lord? Who may stand in his holy place? [4]He who has clean hands and a pure heart, who does not lift up his soul to an idol or swear by what is false. [5]He will receive blessing from the Lord and vindication from God his Savior. [6]Such is the generation of those who seek him, who seek your face, O God of Jacob.
[7]Lift up your heads. O you gates; be lifted up, you ancient doors, that the King of glory may come in. [8]Who is this King of glory? The Lord strong and mighty, the Lord mighty in battle. [9]Lift up your heads, O you gates; lift them up, you ancient doors, that the King of glory may come in. [10]Who is he, this King of glory? The Lord Almighty—he is the King of glory.

*Isaiah 6*

[1]In the year that King Uzziah died, I saw the Lord seated on a throne, high and exalted, and the train of his robe filled the temple. [2]Above him were seraphs, each with six wings: With two wings they covered their faces, with two they covered their feet, and with two they were flying. [3]And they were calling to one another:
"Holy, holy, holy is the Lord Almighty;
the whole earth is full of his glory."
[4]At the sound of their voices the doorposts and thresholds shook and the temple was filled with smoke.
[5]"Woe to me!" I cried. "I am ruined! For I am a man of unclean lips, and I live among a people of unclean lips, and my eyes have seen the King, the Lord Almighty."
[6]Then one of the seraphs flew to me with a live coal in his hand, which he had taken with tongs from the altar. [7]With it he touched my mouth

and said, "See, this has touched your lips; your guilt is taken away and your sin atoned for."

[8]Then I heard the voice of the Lord saying, "Whom shall I send? And who will go for us?" And I said, "Here am I. Send me!"

[9]He said, "Go and tell this people:
'Be ever hearing, but never
understanding;
be ever seeing, but never
perceiving.'
[10]Make the heart of this people
calloused;
make their ears dull
and close their eyes.
Otherwise they might see with their eyes,
hear with their ears,
understand with their hearts,
and turn and be healed."
[11]Then I said, "For how long, O Lord?" And he answered:
"Until the cities lie ruined
and without inhabitant,
until the houses are left deserted
and the fields ruined and ravaged,
[12]until the Lord has sent everyone far away
and the land is utterly forsaken.
[13]And though a tenth remains in the land,
it will again be laid waste.
But as the terebinth and oak
leave stumps when they are cut down,
so the holy seed will be the stump in the land."

*Hebrews 12:28-29*

[28]Therefore, since we are receiving a kingdom that cannot be shaken, let us be thankful, and so worship God acceptably with reverence and awe, [29]for our "God is a consuming fire."

You probably don't automatically think of worship as one of the great beliefs of the Christian faith. But worship is at the heart of our faith and, if we are living the Christian life, at the heart of our lives as well. The worship of God takes many forms in the Bible, just as it does across the world today. Sometimes the congregation is small and the preacher a layman; sometimes the congregation is in the thousands and is accompanied by an orchestra; sometimes the mood is ecstatic and sometimes it is contemplative. I want to suggest that three things are necessary for real worship to occur, no matter the size, style, or culture of the congregation.

I.

The first thing necessary for worship is *recognition*. We recognize in worship that God has a claim and that we have a need.

God's claim on us derives from two fundamental facts: God made us, and God has redeemed us. The 100$^{th}$ Psalm says it well: "Lord, you have made us, and we are yours." Paul, referring to the salvation we have through the cross of Christ, says, "You are not your own, you are bought with a price."

We're not talking about worshipping God Goodwrench, or the Big Daddy, or some kind of Cosmic Buddy. We're talking about coming into the presence of a holy God, the King of Glory, the Creator and Redeemer, the One, the only One, who is without beginning and without end. Well does the writer of Hebrews admonish us to worship God acceptably with reverence and awe.

Think of those in the Scriptures who experienced God and of the awesome reality of that experience: Moses had to take off his shoes. He was on holy ground. Job said, "My ears had heard of you but now my eyes have seen you. Therefore I despise myself and repent in dust and ashes." And Isaiah said, "I am ruined: My eyes have seen the King, the Lord Almighty." When Thomas saw the resurrected Jesus and knew then the truth what he could not accept before, he exclaimed "My Lord and my God!" And when in the first chapter of Revelation John the Elder sees Christ he says, "I fell at his feet as though dead."

To worship God is to recognize what kind of God it is that we worship and to know that we do not just walk casually into his presence. I heard a story years ago of a group of American college students who were touring one of the great cathedrals of Europe. They were being led by one of the continent's most accomplished organists. They came to a large beautiful pipe organ and gathered in closely as the organist explained, with a touch of awe in his voice, "This one was played by Johann Sebastian Bach himself." One of the students responded, "Could I play it? What does it sound like?" The astonished organist and guide said, "Madam, I have never presumed to play it. It was played by Bach."

To worship God we begin by recognizing that God has a claim on us, and by recognizing also that we have a need. Isaiah knew this. In verse 5 he laments, "Woe is me! I am ruined! For I am a man of unclean lips and I live among a people of unclean lips." Then the seraph flew over to him, touched his lips with a live coal, and pronounced that his guilt was taken away and his sin atoned for.

We come also in need of doing something with our guilt and our sin. And we need to do something with our hurt. One of the most perceptive remarks I heard in seminary was the reminder to remember that *everybody* in the pews on Sunday morning is hurting somewhere. We come together this morning hoping in some way to reach up to God, but hoping also that God will reach down to us.

We may think that people in earlier days had different problems than we do, but I can safely assure you that all the people who have worshiped God through the ages have had many of the same needs. They are concerned about their loved ones, especially their loved ones who are sick. Think of how many times people came to Jesus needing someone to be healed—Jarius, the synagogue ruler, whose daughter was dying; the Roman centurion whose child was sick; the man lowered through the roof by friends who obviously cared deeply for him; Simon Peter's mother–in–law, who was in bed with a fever. On and on the list goes. Every congrega-tion has come to worship concerned with the health of its people.

We also come needing assurance for the future, needing a sense of belonging, needing the nurture of fellowship. There is a passage in John Steinbeck's novel, *The Grapes of Wrath*, that is worth quoting. The novel deals with the move west by masses of displaced and disadvantaged persons during the Great Depression. Steinbeck writes, "And because they were lonely and perplexed, because they had all come from a place of sadness and worry and defeat, and because they were all going to a new mysterious place, they huddled together."

Isn't that something like what we do when we worship. Facing the difficult choices of a difficult world, facing the uncertainty of life or the certainty of death, we, too, huddle together—recognizing both God's claim on our lives, and our needs.

## II.

The second thing that worship includes is *response*. Most Baptist congregations have been aware of that and have traditionally ended their services with a hymn of invitation, or a hymn of response. There are good biblical reasons for that. Isaiah didn't just hear God, he responded to him, "Here am I; send me." Jeremiah didn't just see the hand of God in the coming disaster, he preached it. James and John didn't just listen to Jesus, they followed him. Whether it was Matthew at the tax booth, Nicodemus coming by night, the rich young ruler who couldn't part with his goods, or even the older son in the parable whose brother has come home, whoever it was, Jesus called them to a radical and a public response to his preaching of the Good News.

Clarence Jordan founded Koinonea Farms in Georgia back in the '40's and '50's. It was an inter-racial Christian community that was strongly opposed by the majority of white people. Jordan's brother was an attorney, so Clarence went to him one day to ask him to do some legal work for Koinonea Farms. The project was so unpopular, though, that the lawyer wouldn't touch it. Clarence looked at his brother and said, "You know we both walked the aisle of that little white frame country church, and the pastor asked both of us the same question. Best as I remember he didn't ask if we admired Jesus. He asked if we would follow him?"

We need to take seriously the fact that God expects a response when we worship him. That is the primary difference between preaching and teaching. Teaching is imparting information. Preaching demands a response to God's offer of salvation. There is a song with the words, "There's a line that's been drawn through the ages. On that line stands an old rugged cross." And on which side of that you live and stand makes all the difference—whether we fall down before that cross and see in it our salvation, or whether we walk by and heap scorn upon it.

If worship involves a response to God's offer of salvation, it also involves a response to God's challenge for us to do something with our lives. Abraham Lincoln went to church with a friend one Sunday. Afterwards the friend asked, "What did you think of the preacher?" Lincoln replied, "He was tall and a good speaker." Obviously not the answer the man was looking for, he asked, "Did you like the preacher?" Lincoln said, "No," he honestly did not. "And why not?" asked the friend. To which Lincoln replied, "Because he did not ask us to do anything great for God."

Now I know what some of you are thinking. Everybody can't be a Paul, or a Calvin, or a Luther, or a Lottie Moon. That's true. But do we do the things we can do? Maybe the great thing for you to do for God would be to teach a class, or to help with community missions, or to tithe—that would be a great thing for some of you to try in 1993. Or maybe you could be a Monday night visitor. The list is endless. The world is waiting.

### III.

When we come to worship we first of all *recognize* God's claim on our lives, and then we recognize our own needs. Second we *respond* to God's offer of salvation and to his call for us to do something with our lives. Which leads to the final "R" of worship, which is *re-orientation*. Worship should change us. We should not be the same people going out as we were coming in. A little girl came forward during the invitation hymn and said to her pastor, "I want to redecorate my life." Of course he knew what she meant, but the way she said it wasn't bad either. We do need to redecorate our lives and to re–orient them as well. That's what worship does for people. It sends us off in a different direction. It fills us, it lifts us, it equips us, it gives us strength. Sometimes people wonder, "Is it really possible to change, or to be changed? Can I, by the grace of God, become a different, better person? Is it realistic to expect a total re–orientation?" Let me give you an account of just such a change.

In a previous pastorate someone in the church gave me the name of a husband and wife and two sons who did not attend church anywhere. I called and asked if I could visit them, but we couldn't work out a satisfactory time that week, so we decided we would try to arrange a meeting the next week.

Sunday came and I preached a sermon on tithing. I took the passage in Malachi and preached a simple expository sermon, though with perhaps a little more enthusiasm than usual since I felt so strongly about the subject.

On the way out that Sunday, one of the members, a very successful, middle-aged businessman, let me know in no uncertain terms that he thought poorly of the sermon. I responded, "I only preached exactly what the Bible said." He replied, "Well, you didn't have to preach it!" Then he informed me that he and his family would be leaving the church.

Shortly after he and his family came out, another family whom I had never seen before stopped and introduced themselves. Wouldn't you know it was the unchurched family I had an appointment with the next evening! I prepared for another strong reaction, and thought to myself that we were probably losing another family before they even had a chance to join. You can imagine my shock when the man put out his hand, smiled a broad smile, and said, "Any man who can preach that sermon can be my pastor. You come on out tomorrow night."

Which is just what I did. And before I left this young couple, with two young sons, made a commitment to worship and serve the Lord through our church. Before I left, though, the man asked me a question: "Preacher, were you serious about that tithing business?" when I assured him that I was, and that there wasn't much sense in being baptized if you didn't baptize your billfold, too, he broke into another of his disarming smiles. "We have already decided that we will be tithers as of this coming Sunday, even if we haven't figured out how to afford it yet!"

Talk about a change! He and his family did become members, and tithers, and in only a couple of years he was serving as Sunday School Director. The life of each member of that family had become almost completely re-oriented.

In fact, if we truly worship we *will* re–orient our lives. We will leave the sanctuary with new dreams and new desires. We will see possibilities where before there were only problems. We will know the joys of the Psalmist who wrote, "I was glad when they said unto me, let us go into the house of the Lord."

# 11
# Great Beliefs of the Christian Faith:
# THE CHRISTIAN LIFE—
# ARE CHRISTIANS DIFFERENT?

*Hebrews 13:8*

⁸Jesus Christ is the same yesterday and today and forever.

*John 1:29*

²⁹The next day John saw Jesus coming toward him and said, "Look, the Lamb of God, who takes away the sin of the world!"

*Romans 8:28*

²⁸And we know that in all things God works for the good of those who love him, who have been called according to his purpose.

*1 Corinthians 15:19*

If only for this life we have hope in Christ, we are to be pitied more than all men.

Have you ever thought about the question that is the subtitle of this sermon: "Are Christians Different?" If we picked five people off the street at random, and lined them up in the sanctuary, could you pick out the Christians? What if one was a nicely dressed 30–year–old mother, one a male teenager with long hair and an earring, one a retired gentleman, one a bank officer, and one a college professor? Suppose you were told that three of the five were Christians. Could you pick out the two who were not?

If you've been around much at all you know that you can't

look at people and tell if they are believers or non–believers. You might assume the guy with the earring is not a Christian, but your assumption exposes your prejudice and not his religion. Maybe you've heard what a rounder the old gentleman was in his youth, but people change. Perhaps you've seen the bank officer imbibe alcohol at the bank's Christmas party, but that doesn't put him in one category or the other. That leaves the professor and the nicely dressed mother—and everybody knows all professors are atheists and the young mother is a Shirley MacLaine New Ager. But then you remember that probably the greatest arguments in the twentieth century in defense of Christianity were offered by a professor, an Oxford professor at that—C. S. Lewis. And as for the New Age mother, look around this sanctuary some Sunday morning and see how many young mothers there are doing the old–fashioned thing—bringing their children to church.

The long and short of it is this: You can't always tell a Christian apart by his or her appearance, by their past, by their profession, by their social life, or by any number of other things.

Which brings us back to the question, Are Christians Different? And if so, How? I believe that Christians *are* different because they have the following:

I.

First, Christians have a perfect moral standard. And that perfect moral standard is not a book, but a person: Jesus Christ, who was God-in-the-flesh. The Bible says clearly that Jesus is the Word of God. And Paul emphatically declared, "We preach Christ . . . ." In one of the most telling passages from his great theological work known as the Letter to the Romans, Paul wrote "That if you confess with your mouth, 'Jesus is Lord,' and believe in your heart that God raised him from the dead, you will be saved."

So Christians have a Lord, or in modern lingo, a boss, who is at the same time the revelation of God and the perfect moral measure of a human being.

A couple of years ago a nicely dressed, soft speaking young

man came by the church office. He told me that he was a Seventh Day Adventist minister and that he was looking for a place for a small congregation to worship. Other than the fact that they worshiped on Saturdays I knew very little of the religious beliefs of this group. But I was inclined to help them if we could, and provided that we would not be supporting something contrary to our own beliefs. I asked the pastor to bring me a book outlining their theology and then to return in a couple of weeks to discuss the matter. In some areas their beliefs were not exactly the same as ours, but on the key beliefs that Christians have in common they were very much like we were. The Adventist pastor and I discussed theology and then he closed the matter by saying, "Mr. Benton, we believe in the same Jesus you believe in: Your Jesus is our Jesus, too."

And that is the crux of the matter: Christians have Jesus. Now perhaps someone wants to challenge the issue and points out that all great faiths have had their great teachers or moral leaders. Probably true, but none of them falls into the same category. Mohammed began the Moslem faith, but his title is prophet. The Moslems have never claimed he was God–in–the–flesh, nor that he was morally perfect. Confucius was a distinguished teacher, but no one thinks him to have died for their sins, or to have arisen again. And the New Age folk are perhaps most to be pitied. They think each of us is God!

No other religion has Jesus Christ, who was God–in–the–flesh, who lived a perfect moral life, who died for our sins, and who arose again on the third day. But how does this Jesus make us different? The answer would seem to be that since Jesus is Lord, Christians all worship the same God, and since Jesus is our moral standard, Christians all live a perfect life. Both conclusions, of course, are wrong.

We don't all worship the same God, and we certainly aren't perfect, so what gives? We stray from the path in many ways. We don't always worship God. Sometimes we worship money. Some of us worship careers. Most of us are seduced by comfort. Nor do we manage to measure up to perfection, though we do at least have a perfect standard. Christians are different not because they meet the standard, but because they try for it, and because for the most part we *know* right from wrong, even if we don't always do what is right.

Let me illustrate how this is played out in our daily lives. Not long ago one of our members sold an old pickup to a fellow down the road. It wasn't much of a pickup, its real value being that the engine was good. The next day the purchaser appeared at the member's door and wanted his money back because the truck motor had blown up, so the man claimed, on the way home. In telling me about it, the member knew that he had sold the old pickup "as is," but he also knew the buyer thought he was at least getting a decent engine.

For some people the matter would be cut–and–dried; I have the money; you bought the truck; I never guaranteed you anything; Good-bye. But the member didn't say that. He said he would think it over for a couple of days. When he discussed it with me, he said he had "a moral dilemma."

After thrashing the matter around and seeing not only the legal perspective (an open and shut case, as they say), but also the personal perspective, the member offered the fellow half his money back, which he accepted.

This is where Christians are different. There is a moral dilemma around every corner, and the issue for Christians is not only what is legal or what I can get away with. It is also, What is right?, and What would my Lord have me to do?

## II.

The second thing Christians have is forgiveness. This is not a blank check that lets us by with anything; it is the painful purchase made on a cross by the only perfect human being who ever lived. It is the costly way of dealing with the sin problem.

Although sin is not a popular word, it is a powerful reality. Karl Menninger, the psychiatrist who wrote a book entitled, *Whatever Happened to Sin?*, said that if he could convince his patients that their sins were forgiven 75 percent of them could leave the hospital.

Perhaps no writer has ever captured the insidious working of sin, or guilt, in a person's life like the Russian Dostoevsky in his classic *Crime and Punishment*. The chief character, Raskolinkov, commits a murder and then spends the rest of his days tormented by what he has done, until his life becomes so thoroughly tortured and deformed that he finally self–destructs.

Maybe you think that belief in sin and forgiveness doesn't make Christians any different. But is there any other faith that perceives the depth of sin and the tender magnanimity of God as the Christian faith does? Of course other cultures have codes of right and wrong, but do they offer forgiveness for wrong, or only the promise of punishment?

There is, however, a little catch to the Christian understanding of forgiveness. God does forgive us, yes, but He also demands that we be willing to forgive each other. In fact, in God's eyes, and in the Lord's prayer, the two are linked: "Forgive us our trespasses, as we forgive those who trespass against us."

Some of you have seen the current movie, "Sister Act." In the movie Whoopi Goldberg is a singer in a night club who witnesses a murder committed by her boyfriend, who is a kind of mob figure. When Goldberg tells the police what she has witnessed, she realizes her life is in jeopardy, so they hide her out in a convent, where she dresses like one of the nuns. Needless to say, convent life—prayers and worship—doesn't agree very well with the ex–night club singer. But an amazing transformation takes place when she begins to direct the convent choir. The transformation, however, is two–fold. She changes the style of worship music in a way that brings people in off the street and fills the church. But in the process, she herself is slowly and subtly transformed. Not only is she dressed like a nun, she also begins to act like a nun.

In the end, the gangster who wants her dead sends two men to kill her, but they can't do it because she's a nun. He argues that she's not a nun, she's just Delores, who is dressed up like a nun. But when he goes to kill her himself, she gives herself away. She looks at her would–be assassin and says, "I forgive you."

Of course the story has a happy ending, but it is also a story of personal growth. And it brings to light again the truth—not only are Christians forgiven, but Christians also forgive.

### III.

Are Christians different? Yes. They have a Lord who is the perfect moral standard, and they have and give forgiveness. They also have something else. Christians have hope. They have hope both for this life *and* for life after death.

So often Christians are accused of believing in "pie in the sky bye and bye," of preaching an other–worldly religion to keep from dealing with the realities of this world. But that is not true. The fact that we have hope *after* this life is what gives us hope *in* this life. Otherwise existence would be bleak and meaningless. We would be like the man in a cartoon I saw years ago. He's sitting on a box in a room with two doors. On one door is written, "Do Not Enter," and on the other, "Do Not Exit." Of course, he can't go anywhere. His situation is hopeless.

When there is no hope, life is already robbed of its meaning. Some years ago a hydroelectric dam was to be built across a valley in New England. The people in the small town had to be relocated because the town would be submerged when the dam was finished. Between the decision to build the dam and the completion of the project the buildings, which had made the town a model of the picturesque New England village, fell into disrepair. Nobody bothered to paint anything, nor to fix anything. The once scenic town became an eyesore. Why? One citizen summed it up, "When there is no faith in the future, there is no work in the present."

Christian hope is not a way of escaping life. It is a way of dealing with this life and with its troubles. Not long after the article about my fight with cancer appeared in the *Observer* I received several letters from people who were touched by the whole thing. One came from a young mother who had lost a child, a son who happened to have a twin. She poured out her story on the pages of the letter, expressing her grief, her pain, her questions. But she ended up, not sulking in the room of despair, but expressing a deep and profound faith. Nothing could take away her loss, but what a wonderful hope she had. "I know," she wrote, "that God will take care of my son, and that we will be together again."

Is that "pie in the sky" religion? No. It is the beautiful hope that Christians have that this is not all there is, that if there are only two doors, at least one of them is marked "Exit and Enter." We have a way out, but we also have a way home.

# 12

# Great Beliefs of the Christian Faith:
## PROVIDENCE—IS GOD IN CONTROL?

*Romans 8:28*

[28]And we know that in all things God works for the good of those who love him, who have been called according to his purpose.

*Romans 11:33-36*

[33]Oh, the depth of the riches of the wisdom and knowledge of God! How unsearchable his judgments, and his paths beyond tracing out!
[34]"Who has known the mind of the Lord? Or who has been his counselor?"
[35]Who has ever given to God, that God should repay him?"
[36]For from him and through him and to him are all things. To him be the glory forever! Amen.

We usually discuss the Doctrine of Providence in terms of God's work in three areas: God provides for us in creation; He sustains us in our daily lives; and He has prepared for us in eternity. Those three points would make a nice sermon, but they would miss the fact that it is in the area of Providence that we face some of the most difficult questions about the Christian faith.

How do you feel about this question: Is God in Control? Some insist that He is, but others have trouble squaring that with the facts. If God is in control, then why are newscasts full of horror stories every evening, stories of women being raped, of children being molested, of society being threatened by violence, drugs, a lack of respect for authority, and a breakdown of the very fiber that holds us together? If God is in control, then why Somalia? Why Bosnia? Why Iraq? Why Northern Ireland and South Africa?

The question is not easily answered, nor are others: Why do

prayers seem so seldom answered? Why do apparently good people suffer while so much that is evil goes unpunished? Why are people killed by disease or in tornadoes and hurricanes? It is nice to be able to preach three positive points, but there are some awfully persistent questions that beg to be dealt with.

I'd like for us to meet some of those questions head on this morning as we seek to understand better the world we live in and the God we serve. I propose to do so by asking and looking for answers to the following three questions: (1) Why do most things happen? (2) What is God about, or What is God up to? And (3) Why should we be hopeful?

I.

Why do most things happen? Though we may not realize it many of us operate with assumptions about how the events of life unfold. Some of us think God has already set up the plan and determined what is going to happen, that everything unfolds just as God wants it to, all according to his will. The Moslems pretty much believe this way. A seminary Hebrew professor was telling us about an excavation in Israel several years ago. There were several Arabs on the dig and one young father got word one morning that his little boy had been run over and killed. The professor expected the father to be out of work for the week, but he showed up the very next day. Unable to believe that he was already back, the professor asked, "Didn't your son get killed?" The Arab threw up his hands and said, "God's will," and went back to work.

Before you judge him for being cruel think of some of the things we say when something happens. When I was about ten years old we received word of a tragedy in the family. We had a cousin stationed in Bermuda who had a wife and two boys. The wife and boys went to the grocery store one day, came home, and were unloading the groceries when one of the boys went running playfully by the car and into the street. He was struck by a taxi and died immediately. I remember my father's remarks, not meant to be unkind at all, but meant to explain why this terrible thing had happened: "It was his time to go," he said, "and whether he had been here or in Bermuda or somewhere else, it wouldn't have made any difference—his time was up."

Many people believe that kind of theology, which if true makes us mere puppets and makes of God some kind of monster. If God has already decided who you're going to marry, what your profession is going to be, and how and when you're going to die, then we can sit back and quit worrying and just live out our script. You get hit going home by a drunk driver? That's alright. It was your time to go. You fail that course in pre–med? That's OK. God doesn't want you to be a doctor.

Do you see how life pretty soon becomes the theatre of the absurd if we believe that everything happens because God wants it that way? The truth, drawn from the Scriptures and from experience both, is, in fact, the opposite of that. Most things happen because of human decisions and *not* because God is manipulating things to suit some cosmic purpose that he has not bothered to explain to us yet. God has given us enormous freedom and responsibility for our own lives. We and other people like us—we make the decisions behind most of what happens to us.

Listen to some examples. You read a report in the newspaper: "Young Woman Raped In Park." Notice how easily we can be led to faulty conclusions. No woman is just raped, as if it happens out of nowhere. There is always a man who has done it. "Violent Crime Is Up In Charlotte," as if violent crime were like a garden that had sprung to life. But the reality of what is happening is that more people are carrying more guns to more places and are killing people as if life were a replaceable commodity. Crime is up because of decisions that people make.

You may say, "But I'm a victim." Yes, but you are a victim of decisions people have made. A young man decides to take out his anger. A gun manufacturer wants to make and sell more guns. You decided, along with thousands of others, to move to a large city. The taxpayers cut the budget so that there are fewer policemen on the beat. Presto. Behind your tragedy are decisions made by people.

Sometimes people want to think that there is no element of human decision in many of our tragedies; but if you look closely at most of them, you do not see a great mystery, nor God manipulating the strings. You see almost always human decisions.

A company out West investigates industrial accidents: cranes that fall, airplanes that crash, equipment that malfunctions. Their conclusion is that in almost every case there is at some level a human error: a rivet not put in correctly, wires crossed incorrectly, or something overlooked. In fact, Jesus dealt with this same sort of thing. A tower in Siloam fell and the people, as was common in that day, attributed it to God's hand and as a punishment for those who were killed by it. But Jesus scoffed at this approach and asked if they really believed that the people who were killed were worse sinners than the rest.

You see, accidents do happen; and people do suffer and die all around the globe. But most of the time what happens in our lives happens because of decisions that human beings have made. That is part of the lesson in the beginning with Adam and Eve. And it continues throughout history.

II.

That leads us to the second question, What then is God up to? Where does He fit into the scheme of things?

In his book *Disappointment With God*, Philip Yancey tells of a young man named Richard who had lost his faith. It happened in a Sunday evening service. The pastor asked for prayer for the families of nine missionaries who were killed in a plane crash in Alaska. Then the very next thing in the service, a man was called upon to give his testimony of how he had survived an unrelated plane crash that same week. It was unbearable for Richard to hear all the praises and amens for this man's miraculous escape, attributed to God's timely intervention, while on the other hand nine missionaries had been killed and God hadn't done a thing.

Why doesn't God do something? What is he about anyway. Two things here we need to understand: (1) God does not normally intervene in the circumstances of our lives. He does not generally manipulate events to suit us, or to protect us. And Jesus could not have been plainer on this matter. He says bluntly in John, "In this world you will have tribulation." Being a Christian doesn't exempt you from airplane crashes, tornadoes, or violent people. It has never been that way. Jesus prayed for the cup to pass him by, but he died on the cross. Paul prayed for the thorn to be removed, but he was given grace, not deliverance. Simon Peter was crucified upside down. Polycarp was burned at the stake. And the trail of Christian martyrs continues to our own times with Bill Wallace, Jim Elliott, and Paul Carlson.

How do we make sense of all this? The truth is God does not normally intervene in the circumstances of our lives. Can He? Of course, it's His universe, He can do as He pleases. Does He ever? Yes, I believe He does. There really are miracles—but they are the exception, not the rule. Most of us have not been struck blind on the road as Paul was; most of us can safely rest assured that when we are buried, we won't be popping up again a few days later as Lazarus did. No doubt God has done the miraculous; no doubt He still does; but that's not the way He normally does things.

(2) The second thing we need to understand about God's part is that He does want to make a difference in your life and in mine; but it's an inner difference, not a difference in our circumstances. When Jesus told Nicodemus he must be born from above, He was speaking of spiritual re–birth, not physical. This is where God does most of his work—within us, guiding and shaping our religious formation toward the end that we should become conformed to the likeness of his Son, Jesus Christ. It is the kind of transformation that caused John Newton to give up the slave ship and take up the pulpit. It is the kind of transformation that allowed a timid girl from Virginia, named Lottie Moon, to pour out her life in service in China. It is the kind of transformation that allows some of us to survive the death of a child or the frustrations of a difficult life or the rapid onset of our own feeble mortality.

It is the kind of transformation that allows us to sing, "It is well with my soul," when, in fact, our bodies may be screaming out in pain, or our feelings reeling from the thoughtless, careless remarks of someone who does not know when to be quiet.

It is this slow process of becoming something different on the inside that is the work of God in our lives. It is what Jeremiah meant long before Jesus when he said that God wants to write his covenant on our hearts. It is what Paul meant when he wrote in Colossians, "Christ in you, the hope of glory."

### III.

We have covered now two of our three questions. First, Why do most things happen? Most things happen as a result of decisions made by human beings. Second, What, then, is God up to if he doesn't normally cause or determine the circumstances of our lives? And we have seen how God's objective has always been to transform the inner person and to enter into relationship with us. But remember: God won't force the issue. He stands at the door and knocks; he does not come barging in, sending things (circumstances) flying off in every direction. If these first two questions have been answered properly, then we are compelled by them to go on to the third question: Why should we be hopeful?

There are two reasons to be hopeful: (1) because we have the presence of God; and (2) because we have the promise of heaven.

The presence of God means that we're not in this alone. Paul wrote that "in all things God works for good for those who love him." That doesn't mean there won't be painful days, there will be. But in our pain, our darkness, and our doubt, whether we feel him at any particular moment or not, God is with us. "Though I walk through the valley of the shadow of death . . . ," he doesn't say we won't walk there. He says we won't have to walk there alone.

How can we be sure God will be with us? It's a faith issue. We take it on faith. Goodness knows there are times when our prayers seem to stick on the ceiling and God seems as far away as can be. But the testimony of the Scriptures and of saints through the ages is that God's presence is with us.

Chuck Swindoll recently told the story on his radio broadcast of a young mother who died a tragic death, leaving her husband and small daughter to cope with their loss. That night, after the father had tucked the little girl under the covers and had retired to his own bedroom, a fierce thunderstorm came up. The little girl became frightened and went into her father's room and climbed into bed with him.

"Daddy," she said, "Can I sleep here tonight?" He told her that of course she could. Then she said, "But Daddy, I can't *see* you."

He replied, "Honey, I'm right here. And even though you can't see me, I will be here with you all through the night."

Sometimes we can't see God, we can't sense his presence or know by our feeling that he is with us. But the promise of the heavenly Father, given again through the Son, and effected by the Holy Spirit, is that He is with us, and will be with us, and will be with us to the end.

Finally, we can be hopeful because we have the promise of heaven. Someday we will see the big picture. Someday we will understand. Someday the wrongs will be made right and our why will be answered.

Vance Havner used to explain why it is we don't know more about heaven. He said to imagine a 5- or 6-year-old boy or girl sitting down to supper with spinach as the vegetable. Why do you suppose the mother doesn't tell him/her that there is a big banana pudding waiting for dessert? Because, of course, no 5-or 6-year-old (and some a great deal older!) would eat spinach if he knew there was a banana pudding waiting. That is a pretty simplistic explanation, but it also points to a truth. In this life we have to eat our spinach and drink our milk. We have to take our lumps and weather the storm. But someday it will be different. Because the God, who in the beginning pronounced his creation good, will in the end welcome his creatures home. And that, too, will be good.

# 13
# Great Beliefs of the Christian Faith:
# PRAYER

*Luke 11:1-4*

[1]One day Jesus was praying in a certain place. When he finished, one of his disciples said to him, "Lord, teach us to pray, just as John taught his disciples."
[2]He said to them, "When you pray, say:
"'Father,
hallowed be your name,
your kingdom come.
[3]Give us each day our daily bread.
[4]Forgive us our sins,
for we also forgive everyone who
sins against us.
And lead us not into temptation.'"

It is a great presumption to tell people how to pray. Some already have life–long patterns of faithful, regular practice and need no help in developing a good, solid prayer life. Some wonder, "What's the big deal? You can talk to God any time, anywhere." And to a certain extent, that is true.

But the feeling I get most often from people is that many would welcome some help in their prayer lives, that most Christians, in fact, do not feel like experts in prayer at all. Quite the contrary, many are still praying as they did when they were children. Now there's nothing wrong with children's prayers. In fact, children sometimes put us to shame with their honesty and their deep trust. But Paul said, "When I was a child, I spoke as a child. When I became a man, I put away childish things." Some of us are aware this morning of the need to put away childish prayers. "Now I lay me down to sleep" is cute for a 2– or 3–year–old; but hardly the mark of a mature adult Christian prayer life. Some of us earnestly desire that our prayer lives will be worthy of our high calling, and will be the substance out of which our faith and our commitment to Jesus may grow. So I want us to consider this morning not just how to pray—how to pray will depend on a number of given factors at any one time—but how to develop a prayer life that will lead to, or be commensurate with, a maturing Christian faith.

## I.

The first thing to note is that a good prayer life is the result of a decision, not an accident. You may find yourself achieving a number of things in life accidentally—but prayer won't be one of them. There are accidental, or better, incidental, prayers. The exclamation "O, God!" in a moment of crisis is a kind of prayer. In a time of sudden grief one might say, "Lord, have mercy" or "O, God, help me." Those are prayers of a sort, but they are occasional prayers. They occur only at certain occasions and one would hardly count them as the fruit of a mature prayer life.

I'm not saying that one shouldn't pray in times of crisis, or grief, or stress. On the contrary, Jesus prayed every time he faced a crisis in life. *But*, Jesus had already prayed before the crisis as part of a good prayer life that was engaged in on a regular basis.

Note the opening words of this chapter, "One day Jesus was praying in a certain place." He didn't just find himself somewhere and suddenly *feel* the urge to pray. Much of our problem in spiritual growth is that we think everything is supposed to come as a result of feeling. The Bible never once says Jesus *felt* like praying, so he prayed. It presents, instead, the picture of a man whose pattern or habit it was to go at a certain time to a certain place in order that he might pray.

Prayer didn't just happen for Jesus any more than it will just happen for you or me, or anyone else. How much have you accomplished in any area of your life that wasn't the result of a definite decision? *I have decided* to go to college and become a teacher, or a doctor, or whatever. *I have decided* to go to work with this company. *I have decided* to marry this person and have a family with him/her. The course of your life is not an accident. It is the sum of many decisions that have been made along the way. The same thing is true of your spiritual life. It doesn't just happen. It happens when you *decide* that you're going to do what is necessary to accomplish a given end.

Several years ago, Readers Digest carried the story of a woman who felt that all her time was claimed, and none was left to develop for God. She *decided* to do something about it. She began to get up an hour earlier every morning, to go to a particular room, to sit in a particular chair, and to wait on God. Nothing much happened at first; but she kept on getting up and waiting because she had made a commitment to do so. Eventually something did happen. Eventually the time and the place began to be filled by a presence, and then a peace, and then a holiness. She communed every morning with God. Not because she happened up early one day and stumbled on him. But because she got up early every day and waited for him. She heeded the biblical words, repeated over and over throughout the Bible, "Wait on the Lord." She waited, and God came.

The famous Swiss Christian psychiatrist, Dr. Paul Tournier, when asked the secret of his life's achievements and the reason for a sense of wholeness and peace in his daily life, responded, "I attribute it to a decision I made some 50 years ago, to get up early each morning and spend time listening to God."

Now I need to clear up two possible misunderstandings about prayer at this point. Jesus prayed early in the morning; the lady in the Readers Digest story prayed early in the morning; Dr. Paul Tournier prayed early in the morning. Many spiritual giants through the ages have also made it a matter of practice to pray early in the morning. But it is not essential that your prayer time be at any particular hour. A friend of mine in seminary, who is now a pastor, said that he used to feel intensely guilty about this because he was not a morning person. He slept later than most, but he also stayed up later than most. The best time he found for prayer was in the quiet of the late evening, after everyone had retired and when the world had grown still again. For some people, evening is best. The important point is that a good prayer life is like some other things in life: It is largely a matter of being in the right place at the right time, but you must decide when and where that will be for you. If you're serious about prayer, you need to make some decisions. You need to decide to pray, then you need to decide when and where your particular prayer life can best take place and flourish.

Now let me clear up another matter, and this is a major obstacle for many people: a good prayer life takes time. Not necessarily huge amounts of time, but time. I've read of people who spend 3–4 hours a day in prayer. I could never see myself doing that, but some have done it. But on the other extreme—just 3 or 4 minutes just won't do either! Some of us think prayer is like a drink of water that refreshes. You grab it on the run. But it isn't like that in the Bible. Jesus takes time for prayer. That's why he's up early in the morning. He doesn't expect prayer to be squeezed into the busy day. He knows it doesn't usually happen that way. Prayer isn't going to happen on the road from Jericho to Jerusalem, or in the busy marketplace in Capernaum. It takes time, and if you're going to have a prayer life, you've got to allow some time. And why not? Nothing else much is achieved in life without time. Some work all the time to make payments on a house, a car, a boat, a place at the beach or the lake. Some study all the time to make good grades or to get passing scores. Think of how it is when you're dating someone. Even that takes time. You spend time on the phone, time talking to each other, time doing things together. You build a romance. It doesn't just happen. Even romance takes time.

So if virtually everything meaningful in life takes time, why should we think that prayer and an ongoing relationship with the Almighty can be accomplished in a few minutes on the run, or squeezed in between favorite T.V. shows, or resorted to only in emergencies. Prayer requires a decision, a certain time and place, and then some time to happen: "One day Jesus was praying in a certain place." It wasn't an accident. He had set time aside and made it happen. And it took time. Note the next sentence, "When he finished, one of his disciples said to him . . . ." But until he finished they stood there and waited for him. The world will wait for you, too, if you decide to give time to prayer. Not necessarily a long time—but a regular time, even 10 or 15 minutes a day, set aside, committed to being with God. But it will happen when you decide.

## II.

Prayer begins with a decision to pray; but what about the actual mechanics of praying? What should I say when I pray? This bothers more people than you think. Some of the reasons for the popularity of, "Now I lay me down to sleep . . ." is that it gives us something to say. Some people pray only the Lord's Prayer because at least they know what to say.

But we can take the Lord's Prayer one step further and use it not as the actual content for every prayer we pray, but rather as a model. Surely this is the way it was intended. The disciples came to Jesus and asked Him to teach them to pray. He gave this prayer in response, and if we let it do so, it can be a pattern for us as it almost certainly was for them.

Note that the Prayer begins with God and not the person doing the praying. You might say that it is God-centered instead of self-centered. That is to say that the starting point of our prayers ought to be God and not ourselves. This is the second principle of prayer; prayer begins with who God is, not what I need.

The first third of the Lord's Prayer is focused on God:

Our Father, who art in heaven,
Hallowed be thy name.
Thy kingdom come, thy will be done
On earth as it is in heaven.

Now this is at variance with our natural tendencies, and probably with most of our practices. Our inclination is to begin prayer something like this, "Lord, I need . . ." or "Lord, I feel . . ." or "Lord, help me, give me, grant me, guide me . . ." , etc. In almost every case we pay a scant passing nod to God and then get right on with ourselves.

But that's not what Jesus did. It's not what Paul did either. I was struck last year while teaching the January Bible Study at how Paul begins even his letters by praising God. Listen to this line near the beginning of II Corinthians: "Praise be to the God and Father of our Lord Jesus Christ, the Father of compassion, and the God of all comfort, who comforts us in all our troubles, so that we can comfort those in any trouble with the comfort we ourselves have received from God." Several lines later he writes of "the hardships we suffer in the province of Asia." But he began with God. This is the second principle of prayer I want us to get this morning. First, prayer is the result of a decision, not an accident. Second, prayer begins with who God is, not what I need.

Now why is that? Some believe it isn't necessary. One commentator said flatly that God doesn't expect us to praise Him before we talk with him anymore than a parent expects a child to do so. But that misses the point. We don't begin with praise of God because God needs it or requires it. We begin with God for our sake, so that we realize who it is we're meeting with, and so that we can get some perspective on the scheme of things.

What happens when we do that is two–fold. First, we are comforted when we pause to reflect on the greatness and goodness of God. Second, when we look at God, our own problems are seen in their true perspective. You know from American history what a rough–and–ready outdoorsman Theodore Roosevelt was. He spent many nights of his life camping outdoors in some wilderness here or there. And when he went to bed at night he had a peculiar practice. He would step outside his tent, gaze up at the night sky and scan the heavens for a few minutes, catching the glimmer of far-away stars, the reflection of the moon, the broad expanse of the evening sky, and all of nature's night–time beauty. After he had taken it all in, he was known to sigh a sigh of relief, and to remark, "Now I can rest. I see how big God is." Do you see what happened? He took his focus off himself and put it on God. And when he did, he realized just how great God is, and he saw his own life differently in the scheme of things.

Some of us suffer from belief in a God who is too little. Part of the reason we are so overwhelmed by our problems and our situation is that we don't see God in the picture, we don't see how great God is. We don't take time to ponder the fact that God loves us, has provided for us, and continues to give us strength for the journey. We need to remember that the God we pray to this morning is the God who has gotten us this far, and the God who got the Hebrew people out of Egypt, and the God who brought Jesus out of the grave. We're not spending time with an analyst who doesn't understand us, nor with a dictator whose will we're trying to figure out; but with a God who has made us, who saved us and loves us, and who is unconditionally for us. And to know that, really to know that deep down—to feel that every time we pray, can give depth and meaning and blessing to our prayer lives and to our daily lives beyond.

## III.

There's a third principle involved in a good prayer life. First, prayer is a decision, not an accident. Second, prayer begins with who God is, not what I need. Third, prayer includes the real world I live in.

The second part of the Lord's prayer is very much concerned with the needs of our everyday lives in the real world. Listen to the words carefully:

> Give us this day our daily bread,
> And forgive us our trespasses
> As we forgive those who trespass against us.
> And lead us not into temptation,
> But deliver us from evil.

Look at that hodge-podge of concerns: the food we need, the sins we commit and our need to forgive those who commit sins against us, the temptations we face, and the evil of the world that is all around us. That is a pretty inclusive list. It involves things we can ordinarily do something about (we usually manage to work and pay for our food, we can also forgive those who sin against us); but it also includes things we are very dependent on God for—for help in resisting temptation, and for help in making sense out of life in a world that contains so much evil.

I suppose one of the lessons of this part of the Lord's prayer is that prayer can involve a broad number of things, that we not only can sing, "Take it to the Lord in prayer," but we can actually do that—we *can* take it to the Lord in prayer. Children are much less reluctant about this than we as a rule. If you pray with them you will be touched by their openness and honesty. I remember one of Jonathan's very early prayers. After he had covered everything else, he signed off by saying, "And Lord, don't drop the world while we're sleeping."

With the pressures of work, of finances, of keeping a home together, many of us feel like we're about to drop the world many days. Prayer is one way of learning that we don't hold it all up by ourselves anyway, and that God will help us, even with those daily matters, and especially with those areas where we need a strength greater than our own. One reason, I am convinced, for much of the failure in our lives (especially in the area of temptation and dealing with the evil in the world) is that we do not regularly call upon God to help us. The Good News is that we don't have to fight our battles all by ourselves. The God who promised never to leave us or forsake us is not just standing idly by on the sidelines, but is waiting for us to come to him in prayer to be strengthened, filled, and prepared to face the world.

## IV.

One final principle I leave you, and it may be more important than any of the others: Prayer is as much listening as talking.

In the Readers Digest article, the writer made a point of the fact that she got up early to be with God, not just to talk with God. Much of her time was quiet time—nobody was talking. She was just listening. And Dr. Tournier made the same point: he got up to listen to God. He never said much about talking.

We tend to think of prayer almost exclusively as what is said to God; but we would be closer to a good understanding of prayer if we put more time and effort into listening to God. And doesn't that really make sense? Let me explain it with this analogy. Let's say, for example, that the President of the United States called and said something like, "William, I'm convening a conference here at the White House to discuss the moral climate of our nation and our world. The following people will be present: Alexander Solzhenitsyn, the Nobel Prize-winning author, William F. Buckley, the columnist, Mother Teresa, and former President Jimmy Carter. I'd like you to be a part of it to represent the average Southern Baptist Preacher." So I decide of course to go. Now what do you think I'm going to say? With that notable entourage, I'll tell you what I'm going to do—I'm going to listen. I'm going to hang on every word. And I'm going to try to remember as much as I can of what is said. I'm not going to say much at all. Compared to the wisdom and experience in this gathering, I am as a child. I am thankful just to be present, so I will listen and take it all in.

If God is the one with whom we meet when we pray, does it not make sense then to listen? Surely the great spiritual people of the Bible did. How can the prophets and the apostles say time and time again, "The Lord said . . ." or "The Lord spoke to me . . ." unless they were listening?

The older I get, the greater I believe that listening in prayer is more important than speaking. I can tell you this: If you want to experience what you may never have experienced before, to hear in the quietness of your heart what you've never heard before, if you want to arise from prayer with a peace and a preparedness that will equip you as you've never been equipped before, then take time to listen. "Be still and know that I am God." And in your stillness you will know things you never even imagined.

# 14
# Great Beliefs of the Christian Faith:
## BAPTISM AND THE LORD'S SUPPER

*Matthew 28:16-20*

[16]Then the eleven disciples went to Galilee, to the mountain where Jesus had told them to go. [17]When they saw him, they worshiped him; but some doubted. [18]Then Jesus came to them and said, "All authority in heaven and on earth has been given to me. [19]Therefore go and make disciples of all nations, baptizing them in the name of the Father and of the Son and of the Holy Spirit, [20]and teaching them to obey everything I have commanded you. And surely I am with you always, to the very end of the age."

*1 Corinthians 11:23-26*

[23]For I received from the Lord what I also passed on to you: The Lord Jesus, on the night he was betrayed, took bread, [24]and when he had given thanks, he broke it and said, "This is my body, which is for you; do this in remembrance of me." [25]In the same way, after supper he took the cup saying, "This cup is the new covenant in my blood; do this, whenever you drink it, in remembrance of me." [26]For whenever you eat this bread and drink this cup, you proclaim the Lord's death until he comes.

*Romans 6:4-5*

[4]We were therefore buried with him through baptism into death in order that, just as Christ was raised from the dead through the glory of the Father, we too may live a new life.
[5]If we have been united with him like this in his death, we will certainly also be united with him in his resurrection.

Most Baptist congregations celebrate or observe two ordinances, an ordinance being something that we believe Jesus to have ordained or commanded. The two are Baptism and the Lord's Supper. You might be interested in knowing that some congregations along the way have also celebrated a third ordinance, foot–washing. And they have done so for very good reasons. If you read the thirteenth chapter of *John* you will see that Jesus washed his disciples' feet and commanded that his followers continue to do the same as a sign of our being servants to each other.

Except for some small denominations and congregations, however, foot-washing seems never to have been a widespread practice, perhaps because there is about it too much direct physical contact for people to be comfortable.

Baptists and most Protestant churches have determined to practice two ordinances, although the way we do them, and the meaning we attach to them are often quite different.

We should note also that the Lord's Supper has often been ignored in Baptist churches. Sometimes it is added onto the sermon on the grounds that you haven't really been to church if you don't have preaching, no matter what else you do. Often it has simply been neglected. Not long ago a member of another Baptist congregation said that her church had observed the Lord's Supper once in a 7-8 year period.

Let's look this morning at what we believe about Baptism and the Lord's Supper and at what they can mean for us.

I.

First, both ordinances are symbols, but it would be incorrect to say that they are *just* symbols, as if they somehow didn't matter much. Some of the most meaningful things in our lives are symbols. You hardly ever go to a wedding without seeing an exchange of rings. These rings are symbols of one person's love for another and of a shared commitment to face life together. In other words they symbolize something of utmost importance in our lives.

When Carleen and I were just married we went home to a humble mobile home to set up housekeeping. We hadn't been married over a week or two when we were out in the front yard digging and planting some small shrubbery. In the midst of doing this Carleen suddenly had a stricken look on her face. "I've lost my diamond," she said, almost pale with anxiety. We began to look for it right away—not for the ring, only the diamond was missing. When I said to Carleen, wanting her not to feel so bad about it, "Honey, it's only a ring." I meant that the ring might be gone, but the marriage was still on. Well, Carleen started crying. "You said it was only a ring, but I thought it was supposed to mean something." I explained that, of course, it meant something. It meant I loved her, and would care for her, and that we would have children together and grow old together—all these things. Fortunately we found the stone because my explanation didn't count for much.

Symbols in our lives are not just symbols; they are shorthand for powerful realities. I enjoy watching the Olympics when they're on television and I especially like it when the U.S.A. wins because we get to see the flag raised and hear "The Star–Spangled Banner." It never fails to move me. In truth it's just a symbol—cloth dyed red, white, and blue and music that consists of notes—but what a powerfully moving experience it is!

Then, for one more example, there is the Vietnam War Memorial—a long black wall. Do you remember the first harsh responses to it, the people who greeted it with derision and said, "It's just a long black wall." But you need to stand in front of it only once—just one time, and you know, as you read the names and wipe your tears away, you know that there is something sacred here.

So symbols represent what in reality may be so special, so deeply meaningful, and so important that there is just no other way to say it. And that's the way it is with Baptism and the Lord's Supper. They *are* symbols, but behind them are powerful realities.

Look, for example, at what Baptism represents. It stands for the washing away of sin and, as Paul uniquely put it, for the putting on of Christ. It represents our identification with Christ, who himself identified with us when he was baptized in the Jordan River. And it represents the events of Easter—the death and burial and resurrection to new life of our Lord, Jesus Christ.

Baptism is so important that most Baptist churches require it for membership; but remember that it is a symbol of what has already taken place, of the forgiveness of sin that has been received, of the lordship of Christ that has been accepted, and of the Christian life that has been entered into. Baptists do not believe that baptism is necessary for salvation. We believe that it is representative of the salvation that has already taken place. And since that salvation comes to those who accept it and respond to it, we do not baptize infants, but only those who of their own free will and for themselves profess faith in Christ.

Some people wonder why we insist on immersion. The truth is that for the first forty years (roughly the first half of the 1600s), Baptists baptized by affusion instead of immersion, that is by pouring water over the believer. Study of the New Testament word "baptize" convinced early Baptists that baptism in Jesus's day was by immersion. Since then Baptists have fairly uniformly insisted on immersion.

The Lord's Supper is also symbolic. It stands for the sacrifice on our behalf of Jesus Christ, whose body was tormented and whose blood was spilled as he poured out his life for his people. The Lord's Supper symbolizes what was done for us at Calvary, where Jesus died for our sins. When we participate in it, we accept that death on our behalf.

So we see that ordinances are symbols, not *just* symbols, but representations of the most important events that ever happened in the world and in our personal pilgrimage as the people of God.

II.

The second thing to note about Baptism and the Lord's Supper is that they are rooted in the common things of life: water, bread and juice, fellowship around the table, and sharing.

God takes what is common and infuses it with special meaning. I recall a retreat when I was in college and was youth director at a Methodist Church. We took the kids up to the mountains for the retreat. The retreat became an important part of the spiritual pilgrimage of many of the people participating in it, so we decided to have a communion service. However, nobody had brought any juice, nor any unleavened bread or even homemade bread. And—horror of horrors—nobody had brought any of those little communion glasses!

But we celebrated the Lord's Supper anyway. We went outside and sat in a circle beside a fast flowing mountain stream. We took a few pieces of light bread, blessed it, broke it, and passed it around. We took water from the stream, and poured some into each person's little paper cup; and then we gave thanks for Jesus's death and for the forgiveness of our sins, and afterwards drank the water. Then we were silent for a time. Sitting there by the stream was the most common collection God could have put together: kids struggling with dating and love, bad complexions and self-image, students afraid of what the future might hold, a couple of adults awed by the silence of the no–longer playing tapes and radios. It was a holy moment, and God had made it with common stuff.

Some people talk about different threads that run through the Bible, but certainly one recurring theme is God's use of the common to convey the holy. For Abraham it was a ram, for Moses a bush, for the Psalmist a valley with sheep, a rod and a staff, for Isaiah a worship experience in the temple, for Jeremiah a piece of land, for the apostles bread and wine—all common things, used in a way only God could use them, to convey the uncommon holiness possible all around us.

The water of Baptism, the bread and juice of the Lord's Supper, the fellowship of a meal . . . the holiness of God.

### III.

One further thing we need to note about the Ordinance of Baptism and of the Lord's Supper: They both serve to remind us of precious things we should not forget.

We have little rituals scattered throughout our lives that remind us. We think birthdays are special, so we remind ourselves each year by celebrating the day we came into the world. If we are married, we remember each year our anniversary, and often take out the book of wedding pictures and look back. Sometimes it is a painful reminder because the joy and love that we felt for each other then has withered or died in the intervening years. But sometimes it is a good reminder of how far we've come, of how we had then hardly any idea of the path our lives would take.

Family reunions are reminders, too. They help us to remember that we are part of a bigger organism, that we did not get here by ourselves, and that we do not have to live here apart from others. Reunions remind us of the connectedness of our lives.

Baptism and the Lord's Supper are two powerful religious reminders. In Baptism, we identify with the death, burial, and resurrection of our Lord. Each time we witness someone being baptized we should be reminded again of the events of the Passion, and let them come home to us with freshness. We remember the hopelessness of death without a resurrection. We remember that we serve a God who can bring life out of death, order out of chaos, and love out of enmity. There is much to ponder here.

Then when we partake of the Lord's Supper, we also remember. In fact Jesus commanded us to remember each time we take the bread and drink the juice, to think of what has been done on our behalf, of how indebted we are to our Lord. This is how one of the poets put it:

Beneath the forms of outward rite
Thy supper, Lord, is spread
In every quiet upper room
Where fainting souls are fed.

The bread is always consecrate
Which men divide with men;
And every act of brotherhood
Repeats Thy feast again.

Thy blessed cup is only passed
True memory of Thee,
When life anew pours out its wine
With rich sufficiency.

O Master, through these symbols shared,
Thine own dear self impart,
That in our daily life may flame
The Passion of Thy Heart
(James A. Blaisdell)

# 15
# Great Beliefs of the Christian Faith:
## ESCHATOLOGY—
# HOW WILL IT ALL END UP?

*Mark 13:32*

[32]"No one knows about that day or hour, not even the angels in heaven, nor the Son, but only the Father.

*Acts 1:7*

[7]He said to them: "It is not for you to know the times or dates the Father has set by his own authority."

*Hebrews 9:27*

[27]Just as man is destined to die once, and after that to face judgment.

*Revelation 20:12*

[12]And I saw the dead, great and small, standing before the throne, and books were opened. Another book was opened, which is the book of life. The dead were judged according to what they had done as recorded in the books.

*Genesis 18:25*

[25]Far be it from you to do such a thing—to kill the righteous with the wicked, treating the righteous and the wicked alike. Far be it from you! Will not the Judge of all the earth do right?"

*Revelation 1:17-18*

[17]When I saw him, I fell at his feet as though dead. Then he placed his right hand on me and said: "Do not be afraid. I am the First and the Last. [18]I am the Living One; I was dead, and behold I am alive for ever and ever! And I hold the keys of death and Hades.

*Revelation 21:1-5*

[1]Then I saw a new heaven and a new earth, for the first heaven and the first earth had passed away, and there was no longer any sea. [2]I saw the Holy City, the new Jerusalem, coming down out of heaven from God, prepared as a bride beautifully dressed for her husband. [3]And I heard a loud voice from the throne saying, "Now the dwelling of God is with men, and he will live with them. They will be his people, and God himself will be with them and be their God. [4]He will wipe every tear from their eyes. There will be no more death or mourning or crying or pain, for the old order of things has passed away."
[5]He who was seated on the throne said, "I am making everything new!" Then he said, "Write this down, for these words are trustworthy and true."

Eschatology is one of those $4.00 Greek words, but it gets thrown around a lot by theologians, so you might want to learn what it means. Eschaton is the Greek word for the end, so Eschatology is the study of the end times or of the last things.

Human beings have a natural tendency to want to know how something will turn out. We long to be able to see around the next corner or the next bend in the road. That is partly why we have so many polls at election time: We want to know who the winner is going to be before we even vote. It's why we shake the packages under the Christmas tree: We want to know what we're getting before we get it. We want to see what's coming down the road. That is why so many books are sold that predict and describe the end times. And even though the writers don't know any more than you or I, they do make money off of the general inquisitiveness of a big part of the public.

Perhaps we should begin this morning by separating what we cannot know from what we can know. Then we will focus on what we can know, and will try to understand it better.

I.

For one thing, we cannot know the time of the end. We shouldn't feel left out because of that. In Mark 13:32 Jesus says, "No one knows about that day or hour, not even the angels in heaven, nor the Son, but only the Father." On another occasion, after the Resurrection had convinced even the most skeptical of his followers, Jesus said in response to a question, "It is not for you to know the times or dates the Father has set by his own authority" (Acts 1:7).

Does it not strike you as strange, therefore, that there are so many who believe they have discovered what even the Son of God did not know? And should not the mistakes of this group and of that sect, offering up timetables that have been repeatedly wrong—should not this make us worry?

I was out one afternoon visiting with an elderly lady in my first pastorate. After we had talked awhile, she said, "William, don't you believe we're in the latter days? The Bible talks about "wars and rumors of wars," about children rising up against their parents, and about earthquakes and natural disasters? Now don't you believe these are the latter days?"

Well, maybe they are, maybe they aren't. But the evidence she cited has been pointed out in virtually every generation since Jesus. Yet here we are, making a mess of things as often as not, but still going--probably about as obnoxious in God's eyes as that Energizer Bunny that keeps beating his drum across our television screen. Still going—but for how long? Only God knows that, and Christians it seems ought to be content to let the matter rest there, in the hands of the only One who knows when.

The second thing we cannot know is how. How will God bring about the end? A great many people concern themselves with this

issue and spend much time thrashing about in the book of
Revelation. In my opinion they completely misread the nature of
the book. They magnify the details and miss the big picture.
Revelation was written to encourage Christians who were being
persecuted towards the end of the first century. It was not intended
to serve as a timetable. If it had been don't you think the message
would have been pretty clear to most of us. All the way through
the Scriptures, God has gone to great lengths to get the message
through. When He gave up on everything else, he came himself.

Now does it make sense that he would have hidden the future
in the last book, and that he would tease us with it generation after
generation? Such a view makes a mockery of Jesus and of the
saints through the ages who have given their lives in service to
their Lord. Granted, there is much that is mysterious in Revelation,
much that we cannot understand. But a large part of the problem
is that we approach the book listening for the wrong thing. It was
not intended to be a chart of future events except to say to those
suffering persecution, "Hold on. The struggle is bigger than you
can imagine, but God is going to win in the end." The writer
employs rich imagery and much that is symbolic, but it would be
a shame to concentrate on the fine details and miss the broader
strokes of hope, perseverance, and faith.

Now someone may reply that there are other descriptions about
how Jesus will come again and how the world will end. There are
some remarks to that effect, but you need to understand that the
Hebrew and Greek writers both often used parable and symbol to
convey what is most profound. You recall that so many had trouble
accepting Jesus as the Christ because he wasn't the kind of
Messiah they were looking for. Besides that, almost all of them
believed that Elijah would come back to prepare the way. What did
Jesus say to this? He said John the Baptist was the Elijah they had
been looking for.

It does not pay to draw conclusions too quickly. For centuries
the church stayed away from excessive speculation and proclaimed
that Jesus was coming again and that God would wrap things up in
his own way. The when and how of that we cannot know.

## II.

Let's move then to what we do know about how it will all end up. The Bible teaches us that whenever it ends up it will end up with three things: judgment, destination, and renewal.

The writer of *Hebrews* put it plainly, "A person is destined to die once and after that to face judgment" (Heb 9:27). And then in Revelation 20:12 we are told, "The dead were judged according to what they had done . . . ."

The idea of facing judgment for the choices we've made in life can make us very uncomfortable. All of us have at one time or other spoken the cold, crushing word that cut like a knife. And if our sins were before us this morning I have no doubt that we should all go shrieking into the street.

But how can life have meaning without judgment at the end? I rented the video tapes this week to watch the mini-series "Roots." Most of you saw it in 1977, but for some reason I missed much of it. Watching it, however, makes one strangely ill at ease. If there is a bitterness in some black people, you can understand why. They were captured in Africa like animals, put on slave ships that had horrible conditions, and finally sold off as property in America. One of the surprises of the movie was the portrayal of the plantation owners. I expected them to be cast as hateful, beastly monsters. Most of them were not purposely cruel. Yet that took very little edge off the injustice of the matter. However kind they might be one day, they could turn around the next and sell a child from her parents, beat a man within an inch of his life, or rape the black women with impunity. The sad thing is that even after the Civil War, life for many blacks was hardly any better. They were liable to beatings or even lynchings well into the life–span of many of you sitting here today.

Now if there is no judgment for those kinds of horrors, no judgment for Adolf Hitler's ovens and all who helped to put people there, no judgment for the man who snuffs out life today as if it were nothing—if no judgment, then, pray tell, what sense is there in life?

Written deep in the hearts of our faith is the idea that each person must account for himself or herself. It really does matter how we treat other people. It really does count when we cheat someone in our dealings with him.

The skeptics scoff and say no, but we know better. The doubter asks where God is and if He's sleeping, but we know better.

I read an interesting story sometime back about a poor rural congregation. They had hardly any land; in fact the farmers' fields came right up to the sanctuary walls. They also did not have air-conditioning, so much of the year was spent with the windows open in an effort to catch a little breeze.

It so happened that the farmer on one side of the church didn't care for the church, nor its worship, nor even its God. So to make matters as bad as possible for the congregation, he plowed his fields every Sunday morning at 11:00 A.M. He'd drive up and down the rows with his noisy tractor, caring not whether the church was at prayer or the pastor trying to preach.

All year the farmer did this, and his crop grew until he harvested it in October. He couldn't miss the opportunity to say something to the church so he wrote a letter to the pastor. He argued that obviously there was no God, or He would not have put up with such arrogance, and there certainly was no such thing as judgment because he had shaken his finger in the face of the Almighty all year long and had had a bumper crop in October. The pastor replied with a letter of just one sentence. "Sir," he wrote, "God does not settle his accounts in October."

How we need to hear that this morning. Judgment may not be today or tomorrow, or even in October, but it will be real. And our only hope in getting through it is to have as our Lord and chief counsel one Jesus Christ, who died to pay for our sins, if we will let him represent us. That doesn't mean that there won't be judgment or that our sins will look any better then than they do now. It does mean we won't have to serve our sentence. Only God could have taken care of that, and that is what He's done in Jesus Christ.

III.

The second thing we can know about how it will end is that it will end with a destination for everyone. Some will be in heaven and some will be in hell.

We tend to have gone to extremes in describing both of these destinations. We used to be overly exuberant, and so descriptive that you could feel the flames of hell almost licking at your feet. Heaven used to be so enamored of jewels that we could almost catch the glitter of it.

There is an old story of a saint rushing past with a bucket of water in one hand and a torch in the other. When asked what he was about he replied, "I'm going to put out the fires in hell and burn the mansions in heaven and then see who really loves the Lord!"

The church in the last 30–40 years has largely neglected the reality of heaven and hell, so that people now are almost embarrassed by it. Somewhere in between the lively pictorial imagery of the past and the neglect of the present lies the truth that we do have a destination. Exactly what they will be like, we cannot know. But just because we cannot plot them on a map or pinpoint them on a model of the universe does not mean that they are any the less real.

Some have argued against these realities. In some cases people believe in no life–after death at all. Others say that hell cannot be real because God could never be so cruel. But hell is not evidence of God's nature, it is evidence of our freedom, and the natural consequences of the choices we make.

I believe we have hints of destination in this life. In family gatherings, in moments of fellowship with friends, and in times of unselfish giving we feel something of heaven within us. Just as in times of bitterness, in acts of meaness, and in purely selfish choices we feel something of the isolation and condemnation of hell.

Fisher Humphreys, a Baptist theology professor, portrays the reality of hell with an interesting story. A bank robber was shot to death during a robbery and was "raised" by a man in a white suit who said he was his guardian angel. The angel said he was there to give the man anything he wanted. So he took the robber to a large apartment with elegant furniture, a nice bar, a stereo system, and several beautiful girls. At first the robber was delighted, but eventually he became bored and wanted to be taken to a pool hall.

Not only did he get his wish, but he was excited to find when he went to play pool that he sank every ball on every shot. So pool soon got boring and he asked the angel if he could rob a bank. The angel arranged this and the robbery went off without a hitch. After a few robberies, however, he became bored again. Finally he got to the point that there wasn't anything else he wanted to do.

So he spoke with the angel: "Well, Angel, I'd better tell you something. You see, there's been a mistake. On earth I was a bad guy, see? So I really belong in hell with the other bad guys, see? I mean I don't really deserve to be here in heaven. So send me away from heaven."

"My friend," said the angel, "My friend, *you* have made a mistake. Whatever makes you think *this* is heaven?"

What a tragedy, but one repeated over and over again. C. S. Lewis summed it up this way. There are those who say to God, "Your will be done." And there are those to whom God must finally say, "*Your* will be done."

Now I realize that this doesn't resolve all the questions about heaven and hell. We have not dealt with the destiny of those people who have never heard the Gospel. But that is a question for another day. For the moment it is sufficient to hear the verse that comes from way back in Genesis, "Will not the judge of all the earth do what is right?" (18:25).


IV.


So there are some things about the end we cannot know. We cannot know when or how. But there are also some things we can know. We know that there will be a judgment and we know that there will be for each of us a destination. One final thing we can know: There will be renewal.

The word new is an important word in the Scriptures. In fact the last part is called the *New* Testament. The prophet Jeremiah had spoken of a new covenant written on our hearts. Paul said that if anyone is in Christ he is a new creation. Peter said that God has given us a new birth. The seer in the last book of the Bible saw perhaps the most amazing new of all—a new heaven and a new earth, everything transformed so there would be no more "death or mourning or crying or pain."

How in the world can that be? God knew it would be hard to believe so he gave us hints of this renewal—in the hugs of a long gone family member who comes home, in the resurrection of a dead man to new life, and in the changed lives of believers.

Let me tell you a story of renewal. One Monday evening I had come in especially tired. I had chosen that day to fast, so I hadn't eaten. Nor had I rested. I spent all day going from one hospital to another. At about six o'clock I received a call from a church member. She was tense and appeared to be under stress. She simply said, "Can you come over?" They only lived about a mile from the parsonage, so I got in the car and went right over. What I walked into was a family brawl involving a drunk father, a high school age daughter, and a thoroughly exasperated wife.

The husband was throwing around all kinds of threats, including some aimed at me, and no small amount of some of the nastiest talk I had ever heard. We finally got the daughter away from the scene to spend the night elsewhere. In the meantime the man continued to spew venom and drink whiskey. We tried for hours to coax him into bed so he could sleep off his drunkenness. But he wouldn't go. He lectured us on every subject imaginable, occasionally going outside in the rain to lecture even the dogs.

Finally at about 11:00 o'clock that night he collapsed across his bed. We could finally get some rest. The next morning I was walking out of the house to take Jonathan to school when who should be standing on my front porch but the drunk from the night before. Only this time he was sober and his car was packed full. He told me his wife had told him to leave and he wanted to talk to me. He didn't know where to go or what to do. I agreed to talk to him as soon as I took Jonathan to school.

When we sat down to talk I saw that he was much more than just a monster. He was a hurting human being. He wanted me to call his wife and ask her to take him back. I refused to do so unless he would right then and there call Alcoholics Anonymous for help and ask God to help also. He agreed. He called AA and then we prayed. His wife agreed to give him one more chance. Frankly I felt the situation pretty hopeless in human terms. But do you know what that man is doing today, ten years later? He is teaching the 4- and 5-year-old Sunday School class in a Baptist church. That is renewal! That is the kind of story that can only happen when we ask the Lord to come into our lives and to guide us down the road.

What will the renewal be like at the end? I don't know, but I know that a God who can make a drunk into a teacher of 4- and 5-year-old children will be able to take care of it.

# 16
# A GOOD THEOLOGY
# FOR BAD TIMES

*John 16:33*

³³"I have told you these things, so that in me you may have peace. In this world you will have trouble. But take heart! I have overcome the world."

*Matthew 7:9-11*

⁹"Which of you, if his son asks for bread, will give him a stone? ¹⁰Or if he asks for a fish, will give him a snake? ¹¹If you, then, though you are evil, know how to give good gifts to your children, how much more will your Father in heaven give good gifts to those who ask him!"

*2 Corinthians 4:16-18*

¹⁶So from now on we regard no one from a worldly point of view. Though we once regarded Christ in this way, we do so no longer. ¹⁷Therefore, if anyone is in Christ, he is a new creation; the old has gone, the new has come! ¹⁸All this is from God, who reconciled us to himself through Christ and gave us the ministry of reconciliation.

*(This sermon was preached on Sunday morning, June 10, 1990, when the pastor returned to the pulpit following surgery for cancer.)*

The Psalmist wrote, "The lines for me have fallen in pleasant places" (Ps 16:6), and until four years ago this week that was very much the story of our family. My parents had five boys—born, with the exception of one small deformity, healthy and whole. We all grew to adulthood without ever being directly touched by the tragedy that seemed always to involve other families, but never our own. Although mother had five children, I well remember the dear couple beside us who waited many years before they had even one, and only one; and their little girl died with heart trouble only 17 days after birth.

We grew up at Myrtle Beach and spent most of our summers in the ocean waters. Every year we would hear or read of families coming down to vacation, hitting the water in a burst of excitement, and losing a family member to the ocean's powerful currents. In fact the first church I pastored had markers on either side of the sanctuary's front door, in memory of two boys from the church's youth group who drowned together while on a beach outing. Almost every day of summer we played in the waves. None of us ever came close to drowning.

Through the grades we grew, going to school, playing ball, making our way fairly uneventfully through life—guided (it seemed) by a providential hand that kept us safe. Tragedy came to others but not to us. Pepper Geddings was one of the best ballplayers and one of the finest human beings to come out of our childhood. He was killed in college by the impact of a baseball while playing the game he loved so much. Strange accident, we thought. Four of the five of us boys had automobile accidents as teenagers, and none of us required so much as a stitch or a visit to the doctor. We never thought much about it. Tragedy, disaster, disease, death—it always seemed to happen to other people.

It continued in much the same way as we grew older. We went off to college and to military service, traveled overseas, and went our merry ways. Two families very close to us had children killed in accidents while away at college. We all came home unscathed.

Until four years ago this week. Then it seemed as if all the bad that had never happened decided to happen all at once. In the summer of 1986, Mother was diagnosed with breast cancer and had a mastectomy. The pathologist's report showed that the malignancy was already in the lymph nodes, so she began chemotherapy treatments, which made her terribly sick. She wondered at times if the cure were not worse that the disease.

Later in that same summer, I went into the hospital for what was supposed to be a kidney stone. It turned out instead to be a tumor and required the removal of my left kidney. I came home from the hospital on Thursday, only to learn that my brother Richard (10 months younger) had gone into the hospital with a collapsed lung. The next day the doctors diagnosed lung cancer, with "the biggest tumor I've ever seen in a man so young." On Sunday I went back into the hospital with an intestinal obstruction. Tuesday morning Richard was scheduled for surgery in one hospital, I in another hospital, and mother was too sick from chemotherapy to come to either. As it turned out, the doctors did my surgery successfully, but determined that my brother's cancer had already spread too far for surgery. He was treated instead with massive dosages of radiation.

Our family managed to get together during Christmas of '86, by which time we had begun to mend and were beginning to feel more optimistic about the future. We had survived, and had begun to show signs of recovery. My father gathered all of us in the family room, and had us to join hands for a special prayer: "Let's give thanks to the Lord that we're all still here and able to be together. And let's pray that 1987 will be a better year for our family."

It seemed we had gotten what we wanted. I have on my desk at home a picture of our family from our family reunion in October 1987. Mother is laughing; everyone is happy. We were doing well. The reason I have the picture, however, is that it is the last one of our family together. The next month, on the weekend before Thanksgiving, our youngest brother, Don, was killed in a motorcycle accident in Atlanta. We ended the year that we had begun so full of hope with the biggest loss we had ever felt.

Spring 1988 saw the recurrence of Mother's cancer—coming back in her bones and causing much pain. That summer, Richard had a heart attack and had to have by–pass surgery. He began to improve, even as mother's condition steadily deteriorated. She became worse as her cancer spread, though she fought desperately for life, trying every treatment that offered any chance whatsoever. She suffered until she died quietly in the hospital on January 30, 1990.

Could we put it all behind us finally? Had the bad news really run out? Not yet. As you know, three months after Mother's death from cancer, I went to the doctor with some abdominal pain. The CT scan showed an egg-sized tumor just below where the kidney had been removed three and one–half years before. The doctor's words numbed me: "I'm sorry. Your cancer has come back."

Now, on my first Sunday back after surgery, I tell you all of this not as a plea for pity (please, none of that); but rather to establish our common ground. For almost every family here this morning has been touched by some kind of tragedy, or is struggling in some way to survive and to make sense of life. Some of you have experienced one of life's most trying tragedies: you have endured the death of a child. Some of you are grieving over the recent loss of someone dear to you, and some of you even now are torn by the difficulties of rearing children, of making ends meet financially, of balancing obligations to different generations of the same family.

The issue for us this morning is how to make sense of faith and life, how to put the two together. A faith only for good times or only for Sundays is not much of a faith at all. What are we to do with the bad times, and how are we to get through the tragedies of our lives? In short, where is God in all of this?

I.

I want to suggest this morning that we can begin to make sense of the situation by recognizing three things. First, we need to recognize the facts. Life is a mixed bag of good and bad, and from birth to death we are confronted and challenged at different times by any number of possible difficulties. This is just what Jesus recognized and clearly stated. In John 16:33 he says quite frankly to his disciples, "In this world you're going to have trouble." That was not a curse, nor a prophecy. It was a recognition of the facts. This is the same Jesus who said matter-of-factly in the Sermon on the Mount that God causes the sun to rise on the evil and the good, and sends rain on the righteous and the unrighteous. (Matt 5:45)

And isn't that just the way it is? Can you look at the world we live in and make a case that God grants preferential treatment to his people? If you took a census of people in the hospital this morning, would 90% of them be unchurched, or even unbelievers? I doubt it. If coming to church kept you out of the hospital and the funeral home, don't you think the churches would be full?

Good times and bad times come without respect to a person's religious convictions. The obvious fact is that God's people are not God's pets—at least not in the sense that they are spared suffering in this life. If you want to see that in the Bible, look at the lives of the Old Testament prophets and of the New Testament apostles. Time and again they suffered, and many of them died untimely deaths. If you want to see that in the world today, you need only look around you.

Why do tragedies come to us, then? Basically they come for any of three reasons: (1) Some difficulties come because of decisions we make ourselves. When someone comes in up to his or her neck in charge card debts, overdrawn in their checking account, and with creditors calling night and day, my heart goes out to them. But when they say, "Why is God doing this to me?", I must tell them the truth: "God didn't do this to you. *You* did this to yourself by the decision that *you* made." We live in a world where God has given us wide freedom. We are largely free to choose in life; but our choices have consequences. Often the things we bemoan in life have come as a result of choices that *we* have made. (2) Some of our problems occur because of decisions other people make. If a drunk driver hits you on your side of the road, you're a victim of someone else's irresponsibility. In a world as crowded as this one, our decisions often affect each othe—but they are still *our* decisions, decisions made by people. When young people are sent off to war, God didn't send the war. Rather, people made decisions that led to conflict. (3) A badly needed rain also brings the deadly lightning. Even nature seems caught up in the pain of life, but I remind you to read your Bible. Nature is broken, and creation, says Paul, is also frustrated and awaits liberation.

I am not trying to account for all of the bad that comes our way; but I am trying to show that much of it is not so very mysterious as we might have thought; and I want us to see that troubles and pains come like the rain—falling here and there on the Christian, atheist, and agnostic alike. That's a fact. That's the way it is.

Jesus never wrote a song to our knowledge, but if he had he might have sung someone else's opening line: "I beg your pardon. I never promised you a rose garden." Clearly he didn't. He promised that life would have its troubles. We might make better sense of it, therefore, if we begin by recognizing that fact.

## II.

Second, we need to recognize the Father, and see what God is really like. We believe as Christians that the best picture of God is Jesus Christ. When we want to know what God is like, we look at Jesus. When we do that, when we look at his life and listen to his words, what we find is very much at odds with the theology we often reflect in our words and ways.

Look at Matthew 7:9-11. Jesus says, "Which of you, if his son asks for bread, will give him a stone? Or if he asks for a fish will give him a snake? If you, then, though you are evil, know how to give good gifts to your children, how much more will your Father in heaven give good gifts to those who ask him!" He is pointing out to people who already know something of the love of parents for children that God's parental love for us is even greater than our love for our own children.

Now plug that into some of the things I've heard in my own time of sickness and you'll find that there are a lot of well-intentioned Christians spreading bad theology. Several people have said, for example, "God won't put more on you than he'll help you to bear." Now that sounds like something you might want to say, or even hear; but look at it more closely. God is the subject of that sentence. It implies that *God* is causing your problems! Is that what we believe? Does God go around giving people cancer? There isn't a parent here who would give a son or daughter cancer, or any other disease. What comfort is there then in thinking that our heavenly Father would do what no earthly father would even consider?

If Jesus is the best picture we have of what God is like, then consider that Jesus never afflicted anybody with any disease. He healed the blind, the lame, the palsied, the crippled—but he never caused anybody to suffer from any disease. God wouldn't do that. He's a better parent than that.

Others have said, "Well, preacher, God doesn't make a mistake." Granted, God *doesn't* make a mistake. But the faulty implication, again, is that God has brought this terrible affliction. The Lord told the people of Israel through the prophet Ezekiel (Ezek 18) to stop running around saying things about Him that were not true. I wonder if He doesn't want to say the same thing through the preacher today: Stop saying things that aren't true. Stop trying to explain or excuse things by some platitude like, "Well, it's God's will." You don't know that. I don't know that. And the Bible doesn't say that. Read it from beginning to end searching for God's will and about the clearest statement of it you'll find is when Jesus says (and what better authority could you want!) that we are to love God and love each other. God's will is that all should be saved, and to be saved means fundamentally to follow Jesus and obey these commandments.

Now some will want to come back and quote that verse (and some have quoted it to me already) from Hebrews, "God chasteneth whom he loveth" (Heb 12:7ff.) But "chasteneth" means to discipline. Now how do you discipline your children? Not by giving them a fatal disease. Discipline that results in death is not discipline; it's murder! Discipline that leaves a child scarred and marred for life is not love; it's child abuse. God disciplines his children—yes! But he doesn't abuse them. Remember, the love we feel for our own children is only an indication, a hint, of the even greater love that God feels for his.

Would you have a good theology about God, about what the Father is really like? Then learn from the children, and from that sweet childhood blessing that you've heard, and may have said, all your lives:

> God is great. God is good.
> Let us thank him for our food.
> By his hands we all are fed.
> Thank you, Lord, for daily bread.

Let's recognize the facts for what they are, but let's recognize the Father for who He is, and be comforted with the knowledge that the best parent of all is the heavenly One.

## III.

There is another thing Christians need to recognize in making sense of life's tragedies, and that is *the future*. Christianity is a faith rooted in the reality of the present, but always with an eye toward the future. God's people all through the Bible are drawn towards a time and place that is "not yet." They, and we, are always called upon, it seems, to be patient and wait. No wonder Peter said we are "aliens and strangers in the world" (1 Peter 2:11). The poet George Herbert put it this way,

> "if we rightly measure,
> man's joy and pleasure
> rather hereafter than in present is."
> ("Man's Medley")

It is only literary imagination and utopian zeal that would have us believe that this world is, or can ever be, the best of all possible worlds. The Christian faith has proclaimed from the beginning that this world is passing. It is flawed, and its flaws are fatal. But after this, there will be a new heaven and a new earth, and "there will be no more death or mourning or crying or pain" (Rev 21:4). Not here and now. We must wait.

I close with a story I heard a revival preacher tell years ago. I have seen it in print since, so you perhaps have heard it already. But it says so well what I want to convey. A missionary had served many years overseas and was on a ship coming home. He was alone, his wife having died on the mission field. He was tired. He had poured almost all his life into his ministry. As the ship sailed into port, he was surprised at what he saw—a large crowd gathered on the dock, a band playing, banners strung from pole to pole. He didn't think anybody would notice his arrival, much less welcome him with such fanfare. His heart lifted, until, as the ship moved closer, he was able to read the banners and to recognize that they were not for him after all. They were for a movie star who had been filming in Europe and was returning to the states.

His heart sank, his countenance dropped, and his voice whispered, "Why, Lord? I've served you faithfully all these years. Why no homecoming for me?" And in the pause afterwards he heard, as it were, the answer, "But son, you're not home yet."

Folks, you and I are not home yet. We're still dwelling in the world where you have troubles. And it will be much better getting through these troubles if we will recognize the three things I've mentioned this morning: (1) recognize the facts—life is a mixed bag, even for God's people; (2) recognize the Father—He loves us and would do nothing to us that the best parent among us wouldn't do; (3) and recognize the future—remembering what Paul said, "Our light and momentary troubles are achieving for us an eternal glory that far outweighs them all. So we fix our eyes not on what is seen, but on what is unseen. For what is seen is temporary, but what is unseen is eternal" (2 Cor 4:17-18).

Amen.